PROGRESS The U.A.W. and The Automobile Industry The Past 70 Years

By

John H. Jackson

with

Jason Trout

ISBN: 1-4107-3671-7 (e-book)
ISBN: 1-4107-3672-5 (Paperback)
ISBN: 1-4107-3673-3 (Dust Jacket)

This book is printed on acid free paper.

1stBooks - rev. 06/16/03

Table of Contents

Foreword

I was born on May 13, 1932 in the hills of southeast Kentucky near the borders of Virginia and Tennessee. My father had to ride a horse several miles to pick up a mid-wife and bring her back to our house so that she could deliver me. Back in those days, if you wanted to get anywhere, you rode a horse or walked. When I was born, my father was working as a coal miner for ten cents an hour, and he was happy to get it. We lived in a one room house with no indoor plumbing and we barely got by.

We moved around a lot when I was young. My father was getting work wherever he could to support my mother, my two younger sisters and me. When I was seven years old, we moved to a coal mining town by the name of High Splint, Kentucky. I lived there until I graduated high school in 1951.

I then entered the United States Air Force. I served four years from 1951 to 1955. This was during the Korean War. I returned to southeast Kentucky in 1955 and began working for the K.U. Company. I worked there until September of 1956. Then, I moved to Hamilton, Ohio and began working for the General Motors Corporation on October 1, 1956. A year later, I moved to Marion, Indiana and began working at a brand new GM Fisher Body plant. I joined the UAW Local 977. For the next thirty-eight years, I worked at this plant and served my union.

My grandson, Jason, and I have taken my stories and experiences from those years and compiled them with our extensive research on the history of the union and the automobile industry to present you, the reader, with a book that not only takes a unique look at the relationship between the union and corporations, but also presents you with a firsthand account of what it was like to be an auto worker and a union representative during revolutionary times for this country.

This book will show progress - the progress of the UAW, the progress of the automobile industry, the progress that the union and corporations have made together, and my own personal progress from a poor boy in Kentucky with nothing more than a high school education to a union representative traveling, teaching, and earning a very respectable living.

We have decided to focus on the past seventy years, starting in 1932 just before the famous Flint sit-down strikes and bringing you up to the present where the UAW stands as one of the strongest and most respected organizations in the world.

If you are an advocate of unionism, I hope that reading this book makes you as proud as it does me, having written it. If you happen to be anti-union, I hope that this book can open your eyes to not only the tremendous story of achievement and perseverance of the union, but also the necessity of the union in a capitalistic society that continues to be a challenge for the entire working class of this nation.

I would like to thank all the fine people I had the opportunity to work with over the years. I am proud to tell people that I served my mighty union while working for one of the greatest corporations in the world, General Motors.

May this book both educate and inspire you, for it is only through change that we make progress.

John H. Jackson

Chapter One

I was born on May 13, 1932 in Balkan, a small town in the hills of Kentucky, where my father slaved away as a coal miner and my mother did the best she could to stretch the ten cents an hour Daddy made in order to feed and clothe me and my two younger sisters. We were smack dab in the middle of the Great Depression. Franklin D. Roosevelt was about to take office as this country's President, and 550 miles north, in Michigan, in the cities of Flint and Detroit, the automobile industry was entering a time that would forever change the status and the life of the American working man.

Prior to the Great Depression, unionism was not an important issue within the automobile industry. The auto boom of the 1920's resulted in the recruiting of thousands and thousands of laborers, most of whom were white dirt farmers, southern blacks, or immigrants. These workers were completely naive to trade-union experience, and any grievances were dissuaded by the higher pay scales the auto industry had over almost all other industries. Grievances were also defused by a system pioneered by General Motors called "welfare capitalism" in which workers were provided with savings programs, group insurance, and recreational facilities, among other things.

The largest union in the country, at the time, was the American Federation of Labor. The AFL had decided at a 1926 convention that it would initiate an organizing campaign in the auto industry. However, according to the

1

John H. Jackson

<u>Report</u> <u>of</u> <u>Proceedings</u> <u>of</u> <u>the</u> <u>Fifty-fifth</u> <u>Annual</u> <u>Convention</u> <u>of</u> <u>the</u> <u>American</u> <u>Federation</u> <u>of</u> <u>Labor</u> in 1935, this effort "failed to get beyond the verbal stage." The industry, namely open shop Detroit, already had little reason to fear the AFL since the AFL had dedicated itself to "horizontal unionism" in which, for example, all electricians or all machinists were organized, regardless of their industry. The AFL ignored industrial unionism, the "vertical" organization of unskilled or semi-skilled workers within a specific industry. This failure to unionize was blatantly obvious within the auto industry where unskilled or semi-skilled production workers made up the vast majority of the labor force in plants where automobiles were manufactured and assembled.

Then came the Depression. Auto workers found themselves powerless within an industry that was collapsing. Job security received no mention or attention in the system of welfare capitalism. Work time was slashed. Wages were cut. Layoffs mounted. Workers with years and years of experience quickly discovered that their seniority counted for absolutely nothing. This realization was further affirmed in the call-backs coinciding with an upturn of auto sales in 1933.

At this time, auto workers were basically slaves. A man is always in need of a reliable, decent paying job to care for his family, not to mention himself, but during the Depression there was not such a thing, especially for the unskilled and poor. In the early 1930's, there weren't multiple class divisions like there are today. There were rich and there were poor, and everyone lost money during the Depression. So the poor were dirt poor. They were desperate. They were sick. They were hungry and they were dying. And this was obviously not a secret to owners and management within the automobile industry.

2

So if you were "fortunate" enough to receive or retain a job as an auto worker, the treatment and labor tasks, as well as a simple lack of compassion for fellow man, you would have to face was to be hideous and cruel.

Mercilessly, assembly lines were speeded up to increase productivity in order to restore profit margins. Workers were forced to work at speeds that were literally exceeding human endurance. Management ignored seniority in deciding the order of layoffs and rehiring. Workers over forty faced great difficulty in keeping their jobs and securing employment. The methods of compensation used in the industry were extremely complicated, and workers were rarely fully compensated for the time they put in. Female labor was being substituted for male labor. And the health and safety conditions in the automobile plants were absolutely horrible, to say the least. So, auto workers had a lot to complain about, and complain they did.

Grievances mounted, and although, to workers, it seemed that these complaints were being ignored (and to a high degree, they were), the common voice of the auto worker - the combined roar stemming from the inevitable common ground these laborers shared - was beginning to come through loud and clear. Management heard the roar and found ways to evade the issues. Auto workers began to see unionism as their one and only hope for balance and fairness, and they began to recognize an ally in President Roosevelt's New Deal.

Within the New Deal was the National Industrial Recovery Act (1933). This was one of the measures by which President Roosevelt intended to assist the country's economic recovery during the Depression. The act authorized the president to employ a National

Recovery Administration (NRA) to ensure fair and orderly competition in business. The act suspended antitrust regulations and set codes of industrial conduct. Additional sets of codes were specifically drafted for each of more than five hundred industries, including the automobile industry. However, the Recovery Act proved to be too weak to support labor's large aspirations because it was quite unenforceable and easily evaded by management. Labor representatives fought with little success for the collective bargaining promised by the NIRA. The codes did not help recovery as they were intended to do. Thus, in 1935, the U.S. Supreme Court nullified the codes as an "unconstitutional delegation of legislative power," and the NRA and NIRA were abandoned.

Then, labor's hopes were raised again. The National Labor Relations Act was passed by Congress in 1935. Up until this time, management had been free to interrogate, discharge, and completely blacklist workers with union affiliation, or even workers who may have shown simple interest in the possibility of unionizing. Management even employed spies to keep extremely close tabs on their workers. The most notorious spy system existed at Ford, where workers at the massive River Rouge complex in Dearborn, Michigan were not only spied on, they were physically threatened and assaulted by "goon squads" hired by management. These goon squads put forth a "bloody reign of terror" at the plant, actually injuring employees and no doubt intimidating others. Workers started organizing militantly. Strikes in 1933 and 1934 included factory takeovers, and again, there was no shortage of violence among it all. There were several violent confrontations between auto workers trying to form unions and private security forces employed by, and defending the anti-union stance of, their employers.

There were also a number of noted physical confrontations between auto workers and the police, who were there to protect the economic and political desires of their superiors and factory owners more than they were there to protect the peace. Several historians believe that Congress adopted the National Labor Relations Act primarily to avert greater, revolutionary labor unrest.

The NLRA gave workers the right to unionize without fear of management interference. Through the NLRA, the National Labor Relations Board was created to enforce this right. Management was prohibited from committing unfair labor practices, discouraging union organizing, or preventing workers from negotiating a union contract. The NLRA is also known as the Wagner Act, named for its primary sponsor, New York Senator Robert F. Wagner, and its passage, plain and simple, made union organizing possible. At first, auto companies arrogantly ignored the Wagner Act, confident that the Supreme Court would knock it down as it did the National Industrial Recovery Act. As management waited for what was never to be, workers exercised the rights provided to them by the Wagner Act, and these were to be turbulent times for the auto industry.

In 1933, the American Federation of Labor, utilizing the collective bargaining section of the NIRA, began an effort to organize Detroit auto workers by chartering the United Automobile Workers union. However, leadership within the AFL-affiliated UAW was quite conservative, much too conservative to suit the needs of an auto workers union in the mid-1930s. After three years of work, the UAW had a few toeholds among independent auto companies, but it had failed to make a difference in the "Big Three" - General Motors, Ford, and Chrysler. Auto workers were beginning to feel that the AFL-affiliated

UAW was nothing more than a paper union that did not produce results. Advocates of industrial unionism agreed. Led by John L. Lewis of the United Mine Workers, Sidney Hillman of the Amalgamated Clothing Workers, and David Dubinsky of the International Ladies' Garment Workers, the Committee of Industrial Organization was formed. In the summer of 1936, the CIO freed itself from AFL ranks, and took with it the United Automobile Workers. Under their new CIO banner, the UAW prepared itself to do battle with the auto industry, and this was to be the first test of the theory of industrial unionism.

The UAW, revitalized and restless, decided on General Motors as their first target. UAW leaders considered Walter Chrysler to be the auto company owner most sympathetic to labor since he had climbed up the ranks of Horatio-Alger. Leaders felt that if General Motors could be conquered, Chrysler would soon follow. Ford was thought to be too tough an opponent to consider. Plus, General Motors was vulnerable considering that all bodies for its low-priced and high-selling Chevrolets, Buicks, Pontiacs, and Oldsmobiles were built solely by its Fisher Body division. If a strike was to come, and no labor leader doubted that it would, the closing of just a few selected Fisher Body plants would have an immediate effect, striking (excuse the pun) a crippling blow to the company.

UAW leaders also had no doubt that the strike, when it did come, would focus on Flint, Michigan, the core of General Motors. GM had been founded in Flint, in 1908, by William C. Durant, and in 1936, Flint was the pure definition of an industrial city and a company town.

The first objective of the UAW was to raise consciousness. A veteran trade unionist by the name of

6

Wyndham Mortimer had begun to do so before the UAW had even joined with the CIO, organizing the five (weak) Flint UAW locals into one, Local 156. This had planted the seed of unionism in Flint, but in October of 1936, Mortimer was replaced by Bob Travis. Travis was twenty-seven years old and felt to be more energetic and a more personable organizer than the soft-spoken Mortimer. Travis had, at his side, Roy Reuther - brother of Victor and Walter Reuther. In the years to come, as this book will discuss, the Reuther brothers existed as a dominating force within the UAW, and they would go on to make the Reuther name one of the most respected and well known names in union history. Bob Travis and Roy Reuther, both ambitious and deeply committed to trade unionism, formed a strong partnership, and, using the ground work of Mortimer, they set out to organize and unionize the city of Flint.

In Flint, UAW organizers were facing hostile management and a company town crawling with labor spies, so they did the majority of their recruiting at the homes of workers and at secret meetings. There was also the "Flint Auto Worker," a magazine edited by labor journalist Henry Kraus, which was an extremely essential vehicle for getting the UAW word out. It also printed labor grievances, giving workers an avenue to express their discontent. Travis and Reuther wisely focused solely on the workers in Flint's two key Fisher Body plants, Fisher One and Fisher Two. Knowing that having a large number of union members in those two large, much relied upon plants would give them the leverage to serve up the devastating blow they needed when the time came for a strike. The efforts of UAW organizers were made easier in November of '36 when Franklin D. Roosevelt was reelected in a landslide win. The overwhelming victory was taken by union as a good sign that they had support in Washington.

By December, ten percent of Flint's GM workers had joined Local 156. Most of them had done so in secret to avoid spies, and the majority of the Local 156 members were from Fisher One and Fisher Two. On December 22, UAW President Homer Martin met with General Motors Executive Vice-President William S. Knudsen. In the meeting, Knudsen declared that issues such as job security, seniority rights, pay rates, and the work speed-up, as well as union recognition, were not "national in scope." Knudsen informed Martin that corporate headquarters had no say in these matters and that they would have to be handled on a local level with individual plant managers. After the meeting, Martin was convinced that he had been given a run-around, and he was positive that the General Motors Corporation had no intention of adhering to, or obeying, the Wagner Act. He knew there was to be no serious bargaining with any independent unions. And, he knew that the stage was set for a strike.

However, a decision needed to be made as to what kind of strike to have. In 1930, Flint workers had attempted to close Fisher One with a picket line. That attempt ended with the interference of local lawmen assisted by Michigan state police. Signs scattered, picketers were run down by mounted officers, and the leaders of the strike were arrested and then fired. This time, UAW officials knew that their forty-five hundred members could not sustain a conventional picket-line strike in Flint, the core of the GM Corporation. They felt that an entirely different kind of strike was necessary. So, as the year of 1936 neared its end, UAW officials and members had come to the solution that in order to stand up for their rights, they would, ironically, have to sit down.

John H. Jackson

The Sit-Down Strikes

The idea was both simple and genius. Workers, instead of walking off the job, would stop working but stay at their respective machines. In this way, they were not simply making demands, but they were enforcing their demands by holding company property, valuable company property, hostage. A sit-down strike was not vulnerable to police interference, or at least far less vulnerable than an outside picket-line. And it took away any chance for management to bring in strike-breakers, which was the primary answer of management to any strike problem. Thus, the sit-downers were taking their fight directly to management.

Some historians trace the tactic of the sit-down strike back to stone masons in ancient Egypt, but it became known modernly in Europe in the 1920s and 30s when Welsh coal miners, Spanish copper miners, Italian metal workers, and Greek rubber workers sat down at their jobs. Mass sit-downs in France in mid-1936 resulted in a nationwide general strike. The Bureau of Labor Statistics reported forty-eight sit-down strikes in the United States in the year of 1936.

Auto workers specifically watched three of those quite closely - one in South Bend, Indiana at Bendix Products, which was owned in part by General Motors, and two in Detroit, at parts makers Midland Steel Products and Kelsey-Hayes Wheel. All three were successful in winning worker gains (all be them limited), and this impressed and excited UAW members. However, up to this point, no sit-down strike in the U.S. had been executed on a colossal level with colossal results. A sit-down strike in Flint, in the General Motors Corporation, would no doubt be that kind of strike.

UAW militants were more than ready to strike at Fisher One and Fisher Two. However, on December 28, 1936, a Fisher Body plant in Cleveland, Ohio beat them to the punch. Cleveland Fisher was shut down by a sit-down strike. Bob Travis, Roy Reuther, and other UAW organizers in Flint looked frantically and waited anxiously for an excuse to initiate their strike. When a report came on December 30 that GM was moving the stamping dies out of Fisher One, Travis and the UAW had their reason to strike. By that night, the swing shift had completely taken over the enormous Fisher One plant. A couple miles away, sit-downers had also successfully taken over the Fisher Two plant. As 1937 started, the production of Buicks and Chevrolets had ground to a halt. These were the two widest selling vehicles of General Motors - this was serious. In fact, the three strikes alone, the two in Flint and one in Cleveland, were capable of stopping seventy-five percent of the entire production of General Motors passenger cars. This definitely gave the UAW the leverage to win their fight. And to the UAW, winning meant being recognized as the exclusive bargaining agent of the auto industry.

And a fight it was, even more resembling of a war battle, all-be-it a non-violent one. Sit-downers had to organize themselves with military precision. Once all non-strikers had left the building, the plants were barricaded so that no one could enter. Strikers patrolled the plants. Everyone served a daily shift on a committee, managing such things as defense, food supply, and sanitation. Strike leaders wanted to make sure that their efforts were not perceived by the public as unorganized or violent.

News reporters commented on the absence of "wild-eyed fanatics," and mentioned the sit-downers' organization. A striker at Fisher Two explained to the "New York Times" that "We're just here protecting our jobs. We don't aim to keep the plants or try to run them, but we want to see that nobody takes our jobs..." Strike leaders also had to employ strict discipline to ensure their success. Small violations of strike rules meant extra clean-up and the like. Serious offenses resulted in expulsion. Plant cafeterias were turned into twenty-four hour dining halls, and strikers made their sleeping quarters out of what they had, seats and bodies of cars.

Over the next three weeks, strikers shut down over a dozen more General Motors plants. Shortages in parts caused by these closings resulted in many other plants being forced to close. The total number of idled workers was over 135,000. Yet, the main focus always remained on Flint, the center of the empire of General Motors.

Michigan governor Frank Murphy had taken office just two days before the December 30th strikes began. Everyone was aware that Murphy was a supporter of organized labor. Union forces had been essential to securing his election, and this was no secret to Murphy. He had insisted for years that labor organizing "does not intend to impair anyone else's interests, only to secure its own just deserts." He had also said that collective bargaining was necessary for "the gradual amelioration of gross inequalities and social injustices" that threatened American life. And he was a brilliant man when it came to calming a nervous and frightened public, assuring them there was to be no violence in Flint, that peace and order would be retained. More than anything, Murphy seemed to be compelled by peaceful settlement through negotiation. After a night long strike conference in

Detroit, Murphy made known his New Deal mandate for social justice: "We are to secure for wage earners an effective voice in the arrangements that govern their working conditions by upholding the principle and the right to orderly collective bargaining...Force and violence are not to be tolerated. We want the rights of labor protected and we want business to flourish. The government ought to play a helpful part in adjusting differences and settling controversies. It can do this only in an atmosphere of peace and reason and mutual respect." The great sit-down strike was to demonstrate the importance and necessity of collective bargaining and that the right way to have success, and be heard and understood, was the peaceful way. The obvious and necessary first step was to get the two parties together at the conference table. But, as sit-down strikes started in three more Michigan cities, as well as cities in Indiana and Wisconsin, neither side was budging. Workers had taken a stand by sitting down. No labor weapon had ever been as successful and highly regarded as the sit-down strikes of '36-'37.

As the strike continued, Local 156 set up outside picket lines which helped control the traffic in and out of Fisher One and Fisher Two. This made it possible for strikers to take leave and visit their family and loved ones. Populations varied in the two plants during the strike. Fisher One would have a high as strong as one thousand men and a low of ninety, Fisher Two varied from four hundred fifty to as low as seventeen. The problem for strike leaders at Fisher Two was the big number of married, family men in their ranks. As the strike dragged on for weeks, the staying power of these men was greatly effected and challenged by the worries they had concerning the welfare of their families. The tremendous pressures of the strike were thought to be better handled by single men, which Fisher One had a large population of. Strike population also fluctuated as hopes for a settlement would come and go. When numbers fell dangerously low, militant locals from Detroit and Toledo were called on by the UAW. Overall however, the sit-downers persevered. They maintained a strong sense of community. The men grew more and more aware of the magnitude of what they were doing, and this fed their collective self-esteem, strengthening their commitment to the cause and to one another. The strikers were transforming from nameless, faceless parts of a machine into heroes, not only of American labor, but of civil rights as well.

The public started to recognize the importance of the strike as well, and a large number of citizens rallied together with the wives of strikers to give support on the outside and help the men on the inside. Food was the biggest and most immediate problem. An owner handed his restaurant, which was near Fisher One, over to the union, an example of the rallying support. Dorothy Kraus (wife of "Flint Auto Worker" editor Henry Kraus) directed this "strike kitchen." Three times a day, meals were prepared and delivered to the strikers with the help of union security. Close to two hundred people took part in running the strike kitchen. Food was donated by sympathizers, and also by merchants fearing boycotts of their respective businesses.

Bob Travis and Roy Reuther set up strike headquarters in downtown Flint, in the Pengelly Building. This is where strikers and volunteers worked furiously, raising money, strategizing, and cranking out publicity releases. "Flint Auto Worker" and a paper put out by University of Michigan students called "Punch Press" kept the men inside informed. Organizers and supporters equipped cars with loud speakers to enable immediate communication with sit-downers. Outside picket lines continued to show moral support. Wives of strikers formed a Women's Auxiliary, as well as a Women's Emergency Brigade. The sit-down strikes had become a mobilizing effort unlike anything ever seen within the confines of American labor, and this became even more evident as the weeks continued.

Negotiations between the UAW and the General Motors Corporation were not going well, to say the least. The union had agreed to give up their request to be the sole bargaining agent in return for a GM pledge to negotiate on an industry basis, however the company refused to negotiate anything until the sit-down strikers were evacuated. Union leaders and twenty-seven strike organizers weren't about to do that. They were well aware of the power they held with the sit-down, and they knew the tactic had caught the company with their pants down. Management really didn't have a move other than to negotiate, yet William Knudsen (GM Executive VP) wrote to UAW President Homer Martin: "Sit-downs are strikes. Such strikers are clearly trespassers and violators of the law of the land. We cannot have bona fide collective bargaining with sit-down strikers in illegal possession of plants. Collective bargaining cannot be justified if one party, having seized the plant, holds a gun at the other party's head." Of course, this statement was coming on the heels of the refusal of General Motors to abide by the Wagner Act. This was seen by the union as a classic case of the pot calling the kettle black. Knudsen and GM had, ironically, justified the strike in the eyes of sympathizers with their statement. Liberals of the time, such as Mrs. Gifford Pinchot and The Federal Council of Churches made the argument that the strike, a "technically" illegal act, was caused by management's "sit-

15

down" against the Wagner Act. And Governor Murphy wrote: "I find the employers largely responsible for having forced this powerful weapon on labor...A great injustice has been committed against the workers by the employers in resisting the right of collective bargaining and it has forced the workers to use the only effective weapon they could find, the Sit-Down strike."

Negotiations between General Motors and the unions were suspended as both sides continued to blame the other for resisting all "reasonable proposals." GM was scrambling for something to bring this strike to an end. They had, in the first week of the strike, turned to trespass laws. These laws weren't to be much help due to the fact that workers had entered the plants with management's "invitation," but GM still proceeded to take their petition to the courts requesting an injunction (during the first week of the strikes) to "restrain" strikers from occupying Fisher One and Fisher Two. County Circuit Court Judge Edward D. Black granted the injunction on the same day it was requested, but three days later the UAW called a press conference to make known a fact that the General Motors Corporation had failed to mention, or possibly overlooked in their hurried efforts. Judge Black owned 3,665 shares of GM stock which had a market value of 220,000 dollars. The injunction Judge Black granted immediately became a dead letter. There was an uproar within the general public as well as the union, and this was an embarrassing misstep for GM. The first victory within the battle of the Sit-Down Strikes had been won by the union.

Management continued to scurry for a solution. They turned off the heat and water at the two Flint factories hoping to freeze out or starve out the strikers, but this only caused more problems. A huge street fight broke out resulting with the injuries of twenty-four people. Governor Murphy rushed to the city and called in two thousand troops from the National Guard to maintain peace. The Governor made it clear that violence from either party would not be tolerated. He had been writing and speaking of how he hoped and believed that the two sides were going to be able to reach an amicable settlement without any action from the State, but the situation was growing out of control. Amidst public protests, Governor Murphy ordered relief funds for the families of strikers. He instructed the National Guard troops to remain outside the strike area unless they were called upon, and he refused state help in the serving of over two hundred John Doe warrants against "agitators" and "syndicalists." He declared "There is going to be law and order in Michigan" and 'the public interest and safety are paramount." The press cheered Murphy's quick and decisive action. The Governor was becoming the central figure of the effort to settle the strike. The day after the street fight, which had now been labeled a riot, he called GM V.P. Knudsen and UAW President Martin to his office in Lansing. The Governor told the men: "I want peace and order preserved...I have counseled temperance and restraint. Each side must understand that the public authority is supreme in Michigan. By tradition and choice we are loyal to democracy and its institutions. We must settle this in the American way...No one should wish or attempt to place the Governor of the State in the position of suspending the law of the land. This is not right and he is not going to do it...I want your conversations to continue in a spirit of reason and good faith until you have agreed on a basis of negotiations among yourselves."

This conference between Martin and Knudsen, mediated by Murphy, resulted in the "Lansing Truce." The truce had been arranged in that strikers would evacuate plants on the condition that GM would not resume production during the two weeks of contract negotiations. These negotiations were set to begin on January 18th. However, in the midst of the plant evacuations, word came that General Motors had agreed to meet and bargain with the Flint Alliance. The Flint Alliance was an anti-union group actually started by the GM Corporation with the help of former mayor, and local businessman, George E. Boysen, with the hopes of turning public opinion against the strikers. The UAW was wary of the Flint Alliance from its onset. They viewed the alliance as a group for organizing strikebreakers, and worried that the alliance was interested in, and capable of, promoting violence toward the occupied plants. UAW President Martin saw GM's agreement to meet with the Flint Alliance as an all-out "double cross." He felt that it proved the company's bad faith, and the union immediately disregarded the truce. The two sides met briefly on the date appointed for bargaining only to call off negotiations. Governor Murphy arrived again, to insist that the dispute would not be settled by force. He stated, "This matter will be handled by men meeting around a table and looking each other in the eye."

Positions grew harder and stronger as the stalemate continued. Then the most well known figure in American labor at the time, John L. Lewis, came onto the scene, joining Murphy, Martin, and Knudsen in the spotlight of the strikes. Lewis was head of the CIO, and he saw the sit-down as the way to catapult his crusade for industrial unionism. He was a genius when it came to public speaking and a master at handling and manipulating the press. Lewis was a force to be reckoned with, and he would soon be put to the test as government action within the strikes shifted from Flint to Washington. Murphy and the Roosevelt administration, led by Secretary of Labor Frances Perkins, brought together whom they believed to be the two principal antagonists of the situation, John L. Lewis and GM President Alfred P. Sloan, Jr. These two extremely different men, Lewis a charismatic and even theatrical man intensely driven toward his goal of unionism and Sloan a by the book businessman with a deep hatred for President Roosevelt's New Deal, met for two days of secret meetings. The conferences ended with yet another deadlock as Sloan called off the talks and left, angering everyone including President Roosevelt. Sloan consistently refused to bargain with a "group that holds our plants for ransom without regard to law or justice." In reaction, Lewis announced to the country that the high command of General Motors had "run away to consult with their allies to determine how far they can go in their organized defiance of labor and the law." Public opinion concerning this exchange was siding with Lewis and the strikers. In fact, a majority was starting to flourish in the public on the side of the union. General Motors, the largest corporation in the world, was failing to uphold its corporate image with their disregard of the Wagner Act, followed by the fiasco with Judge Black, and the violence in the streets. And GM knew that the public would not stand for the bloody consequences that would result from an armed eviction of the strikers. As Governor Murphy had been saying all along, this strike would have to come to a peaceful end.

The fact was, both sides were suffering from the long, drawn out strikes. Workers were without jobs - 88 percent of the GM work force in Flint was unemployed. Relief funds were greater than they had been during the darkest days of the Depression. The GM Corporation was suffering in that its monthly output of cars in January was down to fifty thousand, a huge difference from its projected production of 220,000. Yet, still, neither side was budging, and tension continued to build. On January 25th, violent incidents occurred at a plant in Anderson, Indiana. More violence came at a plant in Saginaw, Michigan on January 27th. The great Sit-Down Strike was coming to its climax.

On January 28th, General Motors went to the courts once again, requesting another injunction to order strikers out of the plants. Meanwhile, strike leaders were planning their own dramatic move. UAW strategists, led by Bob Travis and Roy Reuther, plotted to capture Chevrolet Four, a factory in Flint that manufactured all Chevrolet engines. They wanted to send the message to GM that not only was the union retaining its initiative, but that no GM properties were safe from the seizure of a sit-down. The UAW had concocted a brilliant and daring plan. Knowing that Chevrolet Four was heavily guarded by GM police, strike leaders began to "secretly" reveal their plan to auto workers whom union counterintelligence had identified as company spies. However, the plan they revealed to these spies was their false intention to target Chevrolet Nine, a bearings plant. Company security took the bait, and on February 1st the diversionary attempt on Chevrolet Nine was met by every guard the company could muster up. Amidst fights and tear gas, the union men were driven out in what appeared to be defeat. However, as the battle ensued at Chevrolet Nine, less than a mile away, other strikers swept through the unguarded Chevrolet Four plant, securing the mighty factory. This perfectly executed plan was the turning point of the strike.

The next day, Judge Paul V. Gadola granted the injunction that called for evacuation of the Flint Fisher

Body Plants within twenty-four hours, and he also imposed a fifteen million dollar fine if the UAW did not obey the injunction. Although the union treasury held nowhere near fifteen million dollars, the injunction did put pressure on the UAW to negotiate. Governor Murphy also felt the pressure to find a speedy end to the strike. As Governor, he was to decide how and when to enforce the injunction. On February 3rd, a massive demonstration took place outside Fisher One showing support for unionists. This served as proof to Murphy, as well as to GM, that an attempt to forcefully drive out strikers would ultimately result in violence, bloodshed, and the destruction of plants. The company finally surrendered to collective bargaining.

The conference was held in Detroit. The union side was represented by John L. Lewis, CIO counsel Lee Pressman, and UAW President Homer Martin. The General Motors side was comprised of Knudsen, John T. Smith, and Donaldson Brown. Governor Murphy acted as the chief negotiator, going back and forth between the two sides, searching for the leverage for a settlement. As talks continued, Murphy found himself under attack in Republican circles of the State Senate. Impeachment talk began as the unenforced injunction hung over the Governor's head. But, as was to become quite clear, Murphy was the perfect man to handle such an enormous situation, especially concerning the state of the nation after the depression. He was a true extension of President Roosevelt and the New Deal, and he will always be revered as a hero of American labor for his actions within the Sit-Down Strikes.

The grueling negotiations went on for days. Eventually, the union agreed to give up possession of machinery in exchange for the company's promise to bargain on specific issues such as wages and working conditions. The union agreed to give up the plants and resume work while these issues were being negotiated. General Motors agreed to take strikers back without prejudice or penalty. The Detroit talks were going well, but the biggest battle within the conference was still being fought over the UAW being recognized by GM as exclusive bargaining agent.

Finally, after eight days of meetings, and a sixteen hour day of final negotiations, the forty-two day Flint sit-down strike came to an end at 2:35 a.m. on February 11, 1937. The two sides had come to an agreement that applied only to the seventeen plants where strikes had taken place, but these were the most important plants in the General Motors Corporation. GM was not required to state that it was recognizing the union (saving face), but it, in fact, was in full recognition of the union. The UAW was given six months to sign up workers before a representational election was to be held. The union won their fight. The Sit-Down Strikes had served their purpose to the fullest.

Later on February 11th, as dusk set in, the sit-downers came out of the plants. The men of Fisher One exited carrying American flags. They were surrounded and joined by an enormous crowd of cheering supporters as they marched two miles to gather with their sit-down brothers from Fisher Two and Chevrolet Four. Then, the crowd, comprised of thousands of people now, held an incredible parade in downtown Flint, marching through the streets and singing their anthem: "Solidarity forever. For the union makes us strong."

Throughout the auto industry, workers sped to UAW locals, anxiously signing up with the union. By October of

1937, just eight months after the sit-down settlement, the UAW had nearly four hundred thousand dues-paying members. They were victorious in the representational elections held in plants throughout the GM Corporation. Independent companies such as Studebaker and Packard quickly recognized the union. After a sit-down strike in April of 1937, the Chrysler Corporation also succumbed to the union. And, although it held out for four years, in 1941 the Ford Corporation also acknowledged the UAW as exclusive bargaining agent. The Supreme Court decision (in April 1937) to uphold the Wagner Act was vital to all of this. Unionization without management interference was the law of the land.

Inspired by the famous Flint sit-down, workers in all types of fields attempted the tactic throughout 1937. The public grew irritated, however. Citizens had accepted that the UAW had no other weapon to use against General Motors in their fight to get the corporation to obey the law, practice collective bargaining, and permit union organization. But once the UAW won their fight, and the Supreme Court upheld the Wagner Act, Americans began to disagree with the necessity of the sit-down tactic. In 1939, the Supreme Court outlawed sit-down strikes as violations of property rights. The days of the sit-downs had come to an end.

The essential and mighty victory in the Flint sit-down strike did not bring an end to the discontent of the auto worker. There was still a great deal of change that needed to come, and there was still a lot to fight for. But, with the victory, and the support of law and government, organized labor was achieving parity with management. The stand taken by the sit-downers was, and still is, the most important act in automobile labor history. Finally, the auto worker could see himself as a strong and vital part of something greater, rather than a nameless, faceless, insignificant part of a machine. Management and the union were still at completely opposite sides of the spectrum, but, even if they were being forced to do so, the two sides were finally dealing with one another. There was still a very long road to equality for the auto worker, but the UAW had given him a voice, a voice that was to be recognized and respected. Progress was being made, and the achievements of the sit-down strike of 1936-37 had set the stage for the amazing amount of progress that was to come.

Chapter Two

In 1941, I was nine years old. I can remember the start of the second World War and not being able to grasp the magnitude of it all. My father, a working man with three children to support, was not called off to war. I recall the long hours my dad put in at the coal mines everyday. John L. Lewis was President of the United Mine Workers. I remember Daddy speaking of organizers trying to unionize the coal mines. I saw for myself truckloads of union men coming into my small Kentucky town, setting up picket lines and attempting to prevent anyone from working. There was extreme violence between union and management. Like the war, my nine year old mind could not comprehend the magnitude of what I was witnessing. What I did know was that it seemed my father worked way too hard and long to make as little money as he did.

As the 1930s came to an end, unionism was firmly planted within the automobile industry. UAW bargaining was already making great strides in providing auto workers fair pay and fair treatment, but there was still a long way to go. The Ford Corporation had still yet to give in to labor organizing. Throughout the auto industry, union and management were at opposite sides, fighting against one another more than they were working together.

In 1939, R.J. Thomas replaced Homer Martin as UAW President, but in that same year something far more serious and relevant began that would affect both the auto industry and the UAW, not to mention this country and the world. With Germany's invasion of Poland, World War II had begun. Less than two years later when the United States entered the war, as will be discussed later in this chapter, the automobile industry would go through a tremendous amount of change.

John H. Jackson

Organizing Ford

The first year of the new decade saw Philip Murray replace John L. Lewis as CIO President. President Franklin D. Roosevelt was reelected. And within the automobile industry, a Ford Motor Strike had begun. In 1937, the seed for organizing Ford had been planted when a former Ford employee who had been fired for union activities, Walter P. Reuther, was caught passing out union handbills with three other men at the massive Ford River Rouge Plant. What was to follow would become one of the most famous incidents in American labor history. Reuther, an executive board member of the UAW, and his three colleagues, UAW Vice-President Richard Frankensteen, and labor organizers, Rober Kanter and J.J. Kennedy were not even on Ford property. They were handing out the handbills on a pedestrian overpass which was near Gate Four of the River Rouge Plant. Yet, the four men were approached by a gang of "toughs" who were employed by the Ford Motor Company and worked for Harry Bennett, Ford's sinister manager of labor relations. Bennett's gang chased down the four men and fiercely beat them. Several press photographers caught the entire incident on film. The attack came to be known as "The Battle of the Overpass."

The incident received national coverage in newspapers and on radio. This was the first attempt to organize the Ford Company, but, more than anything, it showed workers the huge struggle they would have to endure to achieve unionism in Ford plants. Henry Ford had told the "Toronto Star" just a month prior to The Battle of the Overpass that "We'll never recognize the United

Automobile Workers' union or any other union. We'll deal with individual workers."

As the 1940s began, Henry Ford was confident in his ability to continue to hold out against the UAW. Even though it was illegal under the Wagner Act, Ford continued to fire workers for union activity. However, in April of 1941, Ford workers had finally reached the end of their patience. A dispute broke out in the steel-rolling mill of the River Rouge plant when eight workers were fired. The dispute resulted with fifty thousand workers walking out in a spontaneous strike. The huge Rouge complex was completely shut down. Ford tried to keep the company operating by bringing in strikebreakers, but workers remained united in support of the UAW. Union organizers created a car blockade, blocking all roads leading to the plant. The workers had used Fords to shut down Ford.

The plant remained shut down as the strike continued for eight days. On April 10, 1941, the strike was settled. Henry Ford agreed to a National Labor Relations Board election, and he was surprised and hurt when ninety-seven percent of his workers voted for the union. In June, a contract was drawn up, and, at first, Ford refused to sign it. His wife Clara, disgusted with the extreme violence she had witnessed between Bennett's men and strikers, as well as between scabs and picketers, talked Ford into signing the contract. On June 20, 1941, with the signing of that contract, the union had succeeded in negotiating the best contract that had been won from any automaker up to that point, and the UAW was now present in all three of the major automobile corporations.

John H. Jackson

World War II

On December 7, 1941, while German troops were in Russia, Japan thrust the United States into the second World War by attacking the U.S. naval base in Pearl Harbor, Hawaii. On December 11, Adolph Hitler declared war on the United States. President Roosevelt called for an immediate expansion of the armed forces. Men would be called upon to serve their country. Women joined the labor work force, filling in for workers who had become soldiers. And the automobile industry would also be called upon to lend itself to the war effort.

Following the attack on Pearl Harbor, auto workers, including union men, immediately agreed to abstain from any strikes for the remainder of the war. President Roosevelt called a conference of labor, employer, and government representatives in order to end any industrial disputes that could hinder production during the war. Three general points were agreed to by December 23, 1941: 1) There would be no strikes or lockouts; 2) All disputes would be settled by peaceful means; 3) The President would create a war labor board to make final decisions on all disputes not settled by agreements between the parties.

President Roosevelt, in accordance with the three articles of agreement, established the National War Labor Board on January 12, 1942. The President appointed a Board with four representatives from each of three sectors: labor, industry, and public with the objective of settling labor disputes that would affect the war effort. In October of 1942, Congress called upon the President to order a stabilization program that would freeze prices, salaries, and wages. Roosevelt delegated a majority of the administration of wage and salary stabilization to the National War Labor Board. The NWLB became part of a comprehensive program of economic stabilization which entailed controlling civilian purchasing power including prices, rents, wages, profits, rationing, and subsidies. Stated goals for the NWLB were to prevent increases in the cost of living, to keep the migration of labor from one industry to another to a minimum, and to facilitate the prosecution of the war. As the government looked to the auto industry for help in the production of war goods, a new and very different era began for the industry, and the NWLB would prove to be a necessary factor during this new era.

President Roosevelt, well aware of the country's need for an improved arsenal, turned to automobile manufacturers in 1940. Much of the world was already at war, so President Roosevelt approached GM President William Knudsen to acquire the support of the auto industry. Roosevelt knew well the manufacturing capabilities of the industry. With tens of thousands of workers in Michigan plants alone, the President was confident that automakers would be able to mass produce tanks, planes, and a variety of weapons, including ammunition. However, most auto manufacturers were against the idea of producing war goods. But, by the time the U.S. entered the war in December of '41, Knudsen had convinced several automakers to contribute to the war effort. These auto workers would be making goods that they had never produced before. Manufacturers redesigned weapons to make them easier to mass produce, but the biggest challenge for the industry would be the production of complex machines such as engines, tanks, and planes.

31

K.T. Keller, president of the Chrysler Corporation, was approached in the summer of 1940 and asked if his company could make tanks. Chrysler and the U.S. government signed a contract within weeks. The government agreed to build a plant specifically for the project. The plant was called the Detroit Arsenal. The first tank produced by the arsenal was delivered on April 24, 1941. A year later, the plant had produced over two thousand tanks for the U.S. armed forces. In July of 1942, the Detroit Arsenal began producing the M-4 Sherman tank, the war's best known armored vehicle. In December alone, the five thousand workers at the arsenal produced 907 Sherman tanks.

The Ford Motor Company was responsible for one of the best known production achievements of World War II. Henry Ford claimed that his company was capable of producing a thousand planes a day, and he had an idea for a plant that would help make his claim possible. The government knew Ford was a mass production genius. They agreed to construct a factory where the Ford Company would produce B-24 bombers. The plant was to be called Willow Run, and construction began on the enormous project in April of 1941. The largest assembly plant ever built (it included a one mile long assembly line) was completed in September of 1942. An airport was built next to the Willow Run plant so the planes could be flown away. By the end of 1943, the factory was producing bombers at a rate of one and hour.

The auto industry had proven itself to be an essential asset to the country's war effort by lending its remarkable manufacturing abilities. However, these manufacturing capabilities landed on the shoulders of laborers more than management within the industry. Men and women were forced into working harder and faster during war time without any raise in pay. Most of these workers felt this to be a fair, and even satisfying, sacrifice for their country considering the war, but as time dragged on and World War II continued, problems similar to those that the UAW had fought to solve just years before began to arise. Unionism would play yet another vital role in the auto industry during the war.

Autoworkers' wartime concerns included price and wage controls, pay for overtime, and effective procedures for grievances during the no-strike agreement. These concerns brought a hefty workload before the National War Labor Board. Twelve regional boards were established to handle wage stabilization. The regional boards were given authority by the National Board to make final decisions in labor disputes and to rule on voluntary salary and wage adjustments. During the war, wage rate increases were based solely on changes in the cost of living. President Roosevelt had gone to great lengths to stabilize prices during wartime, therefore, increases in wage were strictly limited. Considering the much greater workload that fell upon the auto industry in result of wartime production, grievances did arise.

In order to deal with these grievances, the National War Labor Board utilized the labor relations structure that already existed between employers and unions as result of the strikes of 1936-37. Steps toward wage settlement began with collective bargaining. Where collective bargaining was not possible, the next step was the U.S. Conciliation Service. If disputes continued, cases were brought before the National Board.

As of June 1943, Regional War Labor Boards were addressing wage adjustments by making use of the bracket principle. Wage brackets set the minimum and maximum wage rates for specific occupations. The brackets were seen as a sound economic approach for eliminating wage inequalities. Bracket rates speeded up the processing of cases and greatly reduced the backlog of applications for wage adjustments. Considering the general chaos that accompanies a country during wartime, the government had gone to considerable and successful lengths to accommodate the concerns of both workers and employers during World War II. However, the war had presented new problems within labor industries, especially the auto industry, that would result in the beginning of the Civil Rights Movement in the United States.

Thousands and thousands of men were called to serve their country in the armed forces during World War II. A great number of these men were laborers within the automobile industry which created an enormous void for workers in auto plants, most of which had been turned into arsenals for production of war goods. In order to fill this void, the industry began to employee African-Americans for the first time. Also for the first time, women were given labor jobs in the auto industry. Previously, the small number of blacks who were industrial workers were hired as custodians, or for the extremely unpleasant work that white men did not want to do. Women, up to this point, were deemed incapable of strenuous labor jobs and were employed as secretaries and the like. However, these two minority groups would make great and vital contributions to the labor industries when they were called upon to do so. These contributions, and the obvious contradiction that presented itself as women and African-American workers succeeded in jobs that they could not even obtain before the war, presented legitimate arguments regarding the treatment of minorities in the automobile industry. These arguments would prove to be a precursor to the larger struggle for equality of women and blacks in the United States as the Civil Rights Movement took shape.

A. Phillip Randolph, the only prominent black unionist at the time, worked with President Roosevelt to address the racial discrimination that existed before and during World War II. Black votes were essential to Roosevelt's reelection in 1940, and the President was aware of the great shortage of manpower that existed in labor and defense industries due to the war. In June of 1941, President Roosevelt issued Executive Order 8802 which banned racial discrimination in defense industries and the federal government during the war. The armed forces remained racially segregated, but the auto industry did not.

During the war, over one million African-Americans left the rural south to take jobs in labor industries in the north. These jobs enabled black men and women to earn much more money than they were able to before the war. However, these black workers were met with an enormous amount of resistance upon their arrival to their new homes and jobs. One example occurred in February 1942 when twenty black families were moving into new federally funded apartments near a Polish-American community in Detroit. An angry mob consisting of over seven hundred whites blocked the moving vans and burnt a cross in front of the housing development. When no whites were arrested for the incident, black families became aware of the obvious double standard that existed. These African-American men and women were being called upon to fill a void in production that resulted due to the war, performing a necessary duty for industry and the country, but they were not receiving the support from the public, or the government and law, that they rightfully deserved. Hate strikes were common during the war. There were a great number of noted occurrences in which white workers stopped working in protest of having to work alongside blacks. The UAW opposed these hate strikes. Not only were the strikes a direct violation of the no strike agreements of the unions during the war, but this kind of discrimination was exactly what the UAW had fought so hard to remove from the auto industry in the previous years.

In 1943, there were two hundred fifty racial incidents in forty-three separate cities consisting of violence against blacks over housing and jobs. The worst incident occurred in Detroit, where a riot at an amusement park resulted in the deaths of twenty-five blacks and nine whites. Over seven hundred other people were severely injured during the riot. The Civil Rights Movement was gaining serious momentum in result of these incidents, and would continue to grow tremendously over the following years as will be discussed in later chapters of this book. World War II and the labor movement played an important and pivotal role for the rights of African-Americans in the United States. Black soldiers who returned from serving their country in the war were unwilling to put up with segregation and racial insults in the auto industry. They had sacrificed their lives in the fight against Hitler, and they would be willing to do so again to fight racism in the U.S. The UAW would prove to be a critical supporter for the rights of these black citizens in the coming decades.

The rights of women would also become a serious issue during World War II. The issue that dominated women's lives during the war was how to combine the private sphere of home with the new demands of the war economy in the public sphere. Women were making significant gains in the military, the economy, and, in some instances, even politics. However, these gains were misleading. Policy makers utilized the female workforce for short-term gains during the war, but their long-term goal was to see these women return to domestic lives after the war, reinforcing existing traditional gender roles. Just as African-Americans faced a double standard during wartime, women were facing a double standard of their own.

Due to the critical demand of labor, employers were helping to break down traditional gender roles by hiring women to perform jobs that had belonged solely to men before the war. Women were encouraged by government, media, and industry to serve their "patriotic duty" by taking a job. However, throughout the war, policy makers sent ambiguous messages to women concerning what their proper role in society was. The motive of this ambiguity was the fact that the government feared the long-term consequences of women in the workplace. It was felt that gender roles could be permanently changed if women showed reluctance in going back to their domestic lives once men returned from the war. This political and social fear of women in the workplace was confusing to the working woman. They were told by industry that the American homemaker has the ability and strength to play a vital role in the wartime effort. Yet, at the same time, pamphlets issued by the War Manpower Commission which was established by the government in 1943 to actively recruit women into the workforce, told women that "Even in a national emergency as critical as this, the welfare of our children must be of paramount importance." Basically, World War II had created an immediate economic crisis which left government and industry no choice but to turn to female workers for help, but the message being sent to these women was that they were expected to return to their natural place in the home once they were no longer needed. This was discrimination.

Just as African-American workers in the auto industry had experienced, women faced great hostility within factories. Many male workers felt threatened by women performing the duties that were once performed by men. Sexual harassment was commonplace. Women were hired for the lowest paying jobs or simply paid much less than male counterparts that worked the same jobs. This was horribly insulting, especially considering that women were performing a duty for their country. They were called upon by their country to work, and a large majority of these working women were married with children. Not only did they deserve equal pay and equal treatment, but they deserved to be accommodated with childcare facilities as they sacrificed for the war effort. Once again, the UAW would step in to lend help to workers who were receiving unfair treatment.

By 1944, women constituted more than twenty-two percent of trade union membership. In that same year, Walter Reuther, a leading force in the UAW, pledged to give special consideration to seniority, safety standards, maternity leave practices, daycare facilities, and other problems relating to the working woman. Industrial unionism was lending itself once again to the larger Civil Rights Movement as the UAW pushed for equal rights for women in the workplace. The struggles and accomplishments of workers during World War II had proven to be another giant step for unionism and equality.

Walter P. Reuther and the Strike of '45-'46

In 1944, World War II was nearing its end. President Franklin D. Roosevelt was reelected for a third term as this country's leader, solidifying the fact that the American people recognized the positive effects of the New Deal and backed the President's undeniable support of unionism and equality for the American working man. Unfortunately, President Roosevelt died a year later. Vice-President Harry S. Truman replaced him, and World War II did finally come to its end. And in the automobile industry, a familiar name was emerging as the most powerful and essential force for unionism. That name was Walter P. Reuther.

Walter Reuther was born in 1907 in Wheeling, West Virginia. He was the son of a trade union activist. At the early age of sixteen, he became an apprentice tool and die maker. At age nineteen, Reuther moved to Detroit, Michigan. He joined the Ford Motor Company, but was soon fired for his union activities. He was hospitalized in 1937 in result of the Battle of the Overpass. In 1940, he was badly beaten by strike-breakers and hospitalized once again. His famous union name resulted in infamy among those against unionism, and between 1937 and 1940, Reuther survived two assassination attempts. One left his right hand permanently crippled. Now keep in mind that all of this is the mere beginning of Walter Reuther's fight for the auto worker and the UAW. Also, note that a large number of workers were too frightened to participate in the Sit-Down Strikes even though they

39

were for unionism in the auto industry. The threat of physical harm deterred many men from being outspoken with their support of the UAW. And yet, Walter Reuther had been beaten bloody, consistently threatened, and had two attempts made on his life, not to mention the hostility and resistance union activists faced on a general basis at the time, and he continued to fight harder and harder, standing up for what he believed in at all costs.

What Reuther believed in was progress. He emerged as a leading supporter for social welfare and civil rights for African-Americans and women. This made him extremely popular among progressive circles and overwhelmingly unpopular with conservatives. World War II brought Reuther to public prominence as he received attention on a national level for his plan to utilize unused auto factory space to build aircraft for the war effort. He was offered several different high-level positions in the Federal Government during the war, but turned them down to remain with the UAW. However, he did serve as a frequent consultant to President Roosevelt.

Soon after the end of the war, industrial relations in the auto industry began to break down. The UAW had won recognition shortly before the outbreak of the war. For them, the war was just a truce in the continuing struggle with management. The UAW faced the future with much anxiety regarding their concerns that management sought to weaken, and possibly even disregard altogether, organized labor. At the end of 1945, Walter Reuther led a strike against General Motors that would be the first crucial engagement in the postwar battle between the UAW and the industry.

Reuther, speaking for the UAW, requested that GM reopen wage negotiations now that the war was over. He demanded a thirty percent increase in hourly pay for lost overtime without a change in price. Reuther knew, and argued, that GM could easily afford the pay increase, and his central issue was even larger in scope: whether or not American industry as a whole was prepared to pay sufficient wages and "create enough purchasing power to maintain full employment." The government's wage-price policy limited permission of pay raises to those that did not require price compensation. Therefore, a demand for a wage increase immediately raised the issue of the company's ability to pay. Reuther shaped his strategy with regard to the administration's policy. This is what set Walter Reuther apart from other union leaders. He was a brilliant thinker and a genius strategist (it was no coincidence that this strike began in conjunction with Reuther's bid for the UAW presidency), and he realized that increased wages that forced prices upward devalued the pay increase. He also knew that it created a huge gap between demand and supply. Raising the issue of increased wages without increased prices resulted in great difficulty for Reuther. It frightened and angered management and delayed settlement of the strike. During all the turmoil, Reuther almost lost his bid for presidency, but his plan was brave and ingenious.

The ability of a corporation to increase pay without compensation in price raised issues of corporation profits. Reuther took his argument further than the subject of company prices and profits. He demanded that General Motors open its books to the UAW to prove their inability to pay. This was another brilliant tactic in that it put the corporation on the spot in the public eye. GM denied the right of union or labor to inspect the books or to demand "disclosure of private economic estimates." General Motors claimed that it was protecting American industry, but Reuther and the UAW were gaining public support.

The General Motors Corporation met with union representatives in October 1945 but ignored the key issue of ability to pay. GM President, Charles E. Wilson, claimed that the welfare of the country depended on the ability of enterprise to provide more jobs. He argued that the union's demand was a threat to the financial position of the corporation. Attempting to side-step the issue, Wilson attacked the union by calling them selfish and charging them with "ignoring the national good." Reuther's response to Wilson's remarks included the principle that President Harry S. Truman would assert in a speech two months later: that the nation has a stake in important diputes between labor and management and, therefore, has a right to know the facts, "so that the people may use their power to compel a decision in conformity with the national good." Reuther knew that the UAW had the economic facts on their side, so he issued a challenge to GM to make negotiations open to the public so that the American people could judge "which party is truly concerned with the public welfare - the Union or the Corporation."

Support for the UAW came from Economic Stabilization Director William Davis and Secretary of Labor Lewis Schwellenbach, and from President Truman when, on October 13, 1945, he announced a revised wage stabilization policy and encouraged business to grant increases in pay. Walter Reuther was quick to call this a mandate to GM President Wilson to get back to free and collective bargaining. A Department of Commerce report showed that profits for the auto industry would be $390,000,000 in 1946 and they would increase by seventy percent by the following year, contending that the industry could raise wages without increasing prices. This greatly angered management, especially since the Department of Commerce was designed to represent business and it was now supporting union demands.

The union had been authorized to strike, and, on November 21, 1945, 180,000 members of the United Automobile Workers struck at GM plants. They were joined by another 140,000 members who were already idle and awaiting reconversion. Reuther had forced the strike when, two days earlier, he sent GM a letter offering to arbitrate the dispute. He required an acceptance within twenty-four hours of his initial demand of a thirty percent increase in pay without a rise in prices if the company wanted to avoid a strike. Harry W. Anderson, vice-president in charge of labor relations for GM, replied that the corporation would not "relinquish its right to manage its business. This was not an offer of arbitration but a demand for abdication." With this rejection, the GM strike of 1945-46 began.

On December 20, a fact-finding board created by President Truman met with the UAW and General Motors. GM again asserted that profits and prices were not a proper part of collective bargaining. The corporation announced that they would leave the proceedings if their ability to pay was considered relevant. Toward the end of this preliminary hearing, a messenger delivered a copy of the press statement given that day by President Truman which stated that fact-finders "should have the authority...to examine the books of the employer" because ability to pay was, in deed, very relevant. Still, GM refused to open its books and threatened to withdraw from the hearings.

Collective bargaining continued to fail and the strike went on for months. Tactics of provocation and counter-provocation continued. On March 13, 1946, meetings with a federal conciliator resumed and GM and the UAW finally reached an agreement. General Motors increased wage rates eighteen and a half cents and granted vacations, overtime, and concessions on plant inequities. Issues of price were disregarded in the strike settlement, but the UAW asserted in a statement that "under the current wage-price policy of the government, a price increase cannot be justified on the basis of the flat increase won in hourly rates and other economic gains."

Reuther and the UAW could claim victory. They had exposed the largely unbalanced profits compared to wages within the GM Corporation, and GM had helped the union to gain public support by refusing to open their books. Even more importantly, the UAW established credibility with its demonstration of firmness throughout the strike. Victories for unions over the following years owed their success to the '45-'46 strike and, largely, to Walter Reuther. He had conducted the strike on the basis that "if we do not hold prices while increasing wages, we do nothing more than put workers on an economic treadmill." This argument was at the forefront of all union fights to come.

Reuther was elected UAW President in March of 1946. He would lend his willful, courageous leadership and brilliant strategic thinking to the UAW for twenty-four years as president, securing auto workers guaranteed pensions in 1950, among other achievements that will be discussed later in this book. In 1952, Reuther became President of the CIO. Working in the automobile industry had been transformed from a low-wage, insecure, part-time job, to a career that offered a living wage and hope for the future. Auto workers benefited from this transformation, and owed their new found stature, largely in part, to Walter P. Reuther.

John H. Jackson

Chapter Three

I started working for the General Motors Corporation in1956. I was twenty-four years old. I had just finished serving my country for four years in the United States Air Force during the Korean War. I was shipped to France where I served eighteen months and returned home to my family, in Kentucky, in August of 1955. My wife Zella had given birth to our first daughter, Judy, in November of 1952 while I was overseas. Janet, our second daughter, was born in January of 1955. So, when I returned to Kentucky that summer, to support my wife and our two infant daughters, I began work at KU Electric in Middlesboro, Kentucky. My daddy had stopped working in the coal mines after a falling rock accident broke his leg. None of us had much money. In fact, I suppose you could have referred to us as dirt poor, but we managed and we ate and we were getting by. But I wanted more for my family and I wanted more for myself.

The 1950s weren't the easiest of times for the blue-collar man. The best wages required more than my high school education and with a family to care for, I definitely didn't have the time or money to sacrifice toward furthering my education. I had learned of the progress that was being made in the coal mines by John. L. Lewis and the unions from my father. I became aware of the strides being made in the labor industries as well. My father and Zella's father had both moved to Hamilton, Ohio to find work in the automobile industry in 1955. The union had made automobile plants a place to put in hard work for fair pay. There was still a great deal of progress to be made between management and employees, and

47

management and union, but the work sounded ideal for a man like me. Zella and I moved the family to Ohio just before our third daughter, Sandy, was born.

In the autumn of 1956, I began my employment with the General Motors Corporation. I started work at the GM Fisher Body plant in Hamilton, Ohio. This was an older plant and the union was well established there, so it was a good job and the wage was fair. But I was on hourly pay and I wasn't part of the union yet, so I didn't have much job security. There was a large changeover in the plant in 1957, and I was laid off. I found what work I could around Hamilton until I caught wind of a new Fisher Body plant opening in Marion, Indiana. On Thursday September 27, 1957, my father, my sister's husband, and I drove to the plant in Marion looking to get hired. A co-worker of ours in the Hamilton plant had been hired on in a great position at the Marion plant. Thanks largely to his recommendation, all three of us were given jobs on the spot. My father started that very next day. I drove back to Ohio to gather some clothes and things and to let my family know that we had found good work. I returned to Marion and started that Monday.

I was assigned to work in the shipping and receiving department where I loaded and unloaded cars. With this being a brand new plant, I saw a lot of potential and opportunity for myself. However, the fact that this was a brand new plant also meant that the union had yet to establish itself and organize. So, while I had found a good job that I was much in need of, in the beginning, it wasn't the fairest of jobs. The relationship between management and laborers was impersonal and just plain rough. The men in charge knew we needed these jobs and they took of advantage of our desperation by working us harder than we were physically capable of working.

My first job assignment in shipping and receiving was to load floor pans into a rail car with other parts to be shipped to assembly plants. Another employee and I were assigned to this job. We were told that we had eight hours to have the rail cars ready to be shipped. It was hard work, but it was fair and we were able to get it done. This continued for three days. On our fourth day, the supervisor came to us and said "Today I'm going to separate the men from the boys." He informed us that we were to load the rail cars in four hours rather than eight. This meant we had to work twice as fast as we had been, and we were already working hard and fast. The supervisor went on to let us know that if the rail cars weren't loaded and ready (in four hours) by lunchtime, there would be no reason for us to return from our lunch break. He told us that we would be discharged and we would no longer work for the plant. Now, both my partner and I knew this task was nearly impossible, and I have a good idea that the supervisor knew it too. But I looked at my co-worker and explained that I had three young daughters and I needed work, and that I wasn't aiming to lose this job. So we dug in and started loading. After about a half hour of working at a real steady pace, we could see that the only way there was even a possibility of us getting this job done was if we were to literally run. The pans we were loading weighed over one hundred pounds a piece, and I was already feeling pain and fatigue when we started to run and load. Not only was it terribly strenuous, but it was also dangerous for us to be working so fast with such heavy parts. I was sloshing with every step I took from the sweat collecting in my shoes. We were both soaked and exhausted by lunchtime, but somehow, by sheer will I suppose, we were able to get the rail car loaded. Other car loaders were not as fortunate and they were, in fact, fired. That is the way it was in the early days at a new plant where the union was still trying to establish itself. It was not, by any means, fair. And even though I had pushed my body and completed the task for that day, I knew I could not keep that kind of pace up much longer. It was cruel for management to expect us to work that way, and it was ridiculously unfair for men to be losing their jobs because of management's unreal demands. I decided that day that I was going to run for union office to attempt to keep supervisors from doing to other men what they had done to me and to fight for those who were unjustly losing their jobs.

In 1956, President Dwight D. Eisenhower was reelected for a second term as this country's leader. Eisenhower was a Republican and an extremely different man than Franklin D. Roosevelt. Roosevelt had supported the union movement with the foresight that fair and equal pay and treatment of workers would ultimately result in better business and a better economy. Eisenhower was more of a straight-ahead capitalist. However, President Eisenhower would contribute greatly to the Civil Rights Movement, with inclusion of the labor union movement, during his presidency, all-be-it unintentionally. Eisenhower appointed California Governor Earl Warren as Supreme Court Chief Justice. Warren was a Republican as well, but he proved to be non-stereotypically liberal. In fact, as chief justice, Warren turned the Supreme Court into a body that overturned a century of conservative interpretations of the fourteenth amendment. The Court made groundbreaking decisions in such essential cases as "Brown v. Board of Education of Topeka" under Warren that overturned segregation in schools and throughout the country. Warren and the Supreme Court had made decisions that guaranteed (by law) the liberties of Americans of every class and race against abuse by the government at all levels. This had tremendous effects across the country, including the automobile industry.

The 1950s was an interesting, challenging, and exciting time to be living and working. The lines between classes had diminished a great deal due to the Depression and World War II. Along with these issues of class, race and gender issues were becoming a focus in all corners of the country. Auto workers found themselves part of a struggle for civil rights that was forging itself into the consciousness of all Americans. Leaders of the industrial union movement had laid down a floor plan for fighting by organizing, unifying, making demands, and standing strong. Civil Rights leaders would take their stand and fight in the same way. African-Americans, women, and other minorities had fought for rights within the labor industries. They would now be taking their fight to the government of the United States.

The AFL and CIO merged in 1955 and selected A. Philip Randolph as their first black vice-president. Randolph was the founder and president of the Brotherhood of Sleeping Car Porters and had also worked with President Roosevelt concerning the labor union movement. He had worked and fought for the equality for minority workers since the unions gained prominence within the automobile industry in the 1930s. By the 1950s, as the Civil Rights Movements coalesced, Randolph had achieved several successes in government practices but he still struggled against the continuing problem for blacks in the labor industry. The UAW worked with and supported Randolph and vice-versa. UAW President Walter Reuther had spent his life fighting for the very things Randolph stood for. When Randolph began organizing the "March on Washington for Jobs and

Freedom," Reuther and the UAW provided financial and organizational help. The march took place on August 28, 1963, and within a year, the Civil Rights Act of 1964 was signed.

The United Automobile Workers played an important, supportive role within the Civil Rights Movement. The UAW was based on the fight for fairness and equality within the workplace. Under the leadership of Reuther, this fight included all union members including female and African-American workers. Reuther also took specific stands for the rights of female and black workers. He worked with Dr. Martin Luther King, Jr. regarding civil rights of blacks within the unions. The UAW came to King's aid with financial and legal support when he was jailed for civil disobedience. Along with A. Philip Randolph, Reuther and Dr. King were leaders of the March on Washington in 1963 and met with President John F. Kennedy after the march.

To men like Reuther, Randolph, and Dr. King, the labor union movement and the Civil Rights Movement were one in the same. The achievements of union leaders were a smaller but significant part of the larger struggle for rights of all Americans, especially minorities and anyone experiencing discrimination. Auto workers of all colors had been discriminated against since the industry began. They were still experiencing discrimination more than twenty years after the sit down strikes. Women workers were still struggling for acceptance. Black workers had fought for rights inside and outside of the auto industry and still, in many plants, could not get the pay raises and promotions that some of their white co-workers were receiving. Fair treatment and pay was still an unmet goal for workers of all color and gender. But with the Civil Rights Movement, the country was beginning to change. John F. Kennedy was our President and the 1960s were a time of hope, a time for and of progress. It was time to recognize hypocrisy and take a stand for democracy. The UAW would do just that.

In 1960, I decided to run for alternate committeeman. Committeemen served one year terms at the time. The position of alternate committeeman would allow me to experience things firsthand, and learn how to be an effective union official and also see if it was, in fact, something I truly wanted to do. I served my one year as alternate committeeman and I loved it. The next year I became Shop Committeeman. During my first few years of serving as committeeman for the union, supervision and higher management did everything in their power to try to change me. They wanted me to do things their way and look the other way regarding the problems they were causing for the union. Of course, this was something I would not do. The very reason that I wanted to be a committeeman was to protect the rights of workers and bring change and progress to my plant. Everyday I walked into the factory, it was the same thing: supervisors hassling employees, disciplining them without just cause or for no reason at all. Management and supervision were simply trying to get back at the union for things they didn't agree with. On several occasions, I had supervisors threaten to discipline random, innocent workers if I did not agree to do certain things a certain way. I would take this to higher management who would tell me that the supervisors would be spoken to and that the problem would be taken care of. When I failed to notice any change, I would then go to labor relations who would also assure me that the problem would be addressed. I still failed to see any change.

When I was elected district committeeman in 1961 and 1962, committeemen had only two hours a day to serve as committeemen. This severely limited our time to do union work. As committeeman, it was my job to be the voice of our workers and to be heard by management. I had already been dealing with the run-arounds being given to me by management and labor relations. Now, I was beginning to see that the union did not have a sufficient amount of time on the factory floor to do its job effectively. This made it easy for supervisors to continue with their unfair practices and for management to give committeemen the run-around. They knew that we had our own assembly or loading work to do for the majority of our day. This would also result in my co-workers being angered with me because I simply did not have the time to answer their calls. It was easy to recognize that I was part of a cycle that worked against the union and for management. When a district committeeman or shop committeeman went on call at the plant, they were required to sign in a log book located in their district. They would also have to sign out, and when their two hours were up, the only way they could function as committeemen was to speed up on the production lines and do more than a fair day of work. This is exactly what the union stood against.

As the 1960s began, the United States economy was doing quite well. The country had gotten through the Depression and World War II, and President Eisenhower's eight years had brought major industrial growth. The automobile business was booming, and corporations like General Motors were making profits in the hundreds of millions. Auto workers were not in the dark about the large profits. They were especially aware of profits and higher management salaries in comparison to their own. Laborers were the men and women doing the actual hands on work in these plants, producing parts, assembling, and loading and shipping hundreds of thousands of cars each year. Auto companies were building new plants frequently, and this created problems for the union. Obviously, the new jobs were a purely positive thing, but establishing a strong union presence was troublesome. This meant that management and supervisors could and would take advantage of workers at the new plants, threatening termination for unjust reasons, pushing workers beyond a fair day's work, and giving union executives the run-around - playing them against workers and sending them and their stockpile of grievances back and forth from workers to management to labor relations back to the floor and so on. With every new plant came a new fight for the UAW for fairness. The union had spent years to establish itself within the auto industry. They had extremely large numbers and had gained many rights and benefits for auto workers, but the fight still was not over. With auto companies bringing in exceptionally large profits, the least the UAW expected was fair treatment and the chance for collective bargaining that had been guaranteed to them by law.

President John F. Kennedy took office in 1960. He brought with him hope and promise for the nation. As has already been discussed, his amazing commitment to civil rights led to the signing of the Civil Rights Act in 1964, less than a year after his assassination. Kennedy's presidency also meant strong governmental support for the UAW. In 1961, UAW bargaining brought paid hospital and surgical benefits and improved relief time for workers. Bargaining also resulted in the establishment of anti-discrimination clauses within the auto industry. The union continued to accomplish great things, but problems lied within execution. Even in the sixties, thirty years after the sit-down strikes, management and supervisors at many auto plants were still doing the best they could to sidestep, or simply ignore the union, treating grievances and union leaders with disdain and procrastination and involving themselves in wrongful, and sometimes illegal practices. These battles would be fought at the local level. It would be up to UAW locals to right the wrongs at their individual plants just as leaders like John L. Lewis and Walter Reuther had done on the national level. Those national successes provided a sturdy foundation for UAW locals to fight and bargain from, and these local unions, from presidents to committeemen to simple dues paying members, would use that foundation to fight for the betterment, and ensure the security of, the lives of auto workers.

An essential and important change came as I served as Committeeman in the early sixties. Negotiations between the UAW and the General Motors Corporation resulted in the agreement that committeemen and other union representatives would now serve full time at the plant, meaning that we no longer had to split our time between our assembly or loading jobs and our union duties. This was a big deal, to say the least, and change happened immediately. Before this, supervisors could count on committeeman to be tied up with labor work for the majority of the day. This had kept us from being able to answer all of our calls and it often resulted in frustration toward us from the workers who counted on us for help. Supervisors and management seemed to love the fact that our lack of time to perform our union business had several workers questioning the ability of the UAW. But now, we union representatives were to spend our entire work day answering calls, filing grievances, maintaining communication with all workers, and overseeing all of the action in the factory. I was now able to accompany supervisors on the production floor and ensure that they treated workers fairly. The workers could now see with their own eyes how dedicated we were to them and to the union. This did a tremendous amount for morale, and you could feel the UAW growing and strengthening within our new plant in Marion. UAW Local 977 was established and we were making progress.

However, things were not easy, by any means. We knew that we were fighting the good fight and accomplishing important goals, but the relationship between management and union leaders like myself was stressful and strained. It was understandable considering that it was our job as representatives of the UAW to keep supervisors in line. Supervisors did not like being watched so carefully, and I can understand that, but the UAW envisioned progressing to a time that supervisors and management would not have to be kept in line, a time where workers would be treated fairly, free from harassment and threats. We definitely had not reached that time yet, so we committeemen kept ourselves informed of all the goings on in our specific departments and did not hesitate to come to our workers' aid and call supervision on any and all unfair practices. We dealt with a good deal of contempt and grandstanding from management. And there was also plenty of under the table deals being offered to us to sweep grievances under the rug or simply look the other way every once in a while. I was never a look the other way kind of guy, and I took pride in what we were doing with the UAW, but I had several interactions with supervisors trying to cut a deal. For example, once I was meeting with the department Superintendent regarding a matter of several grievances concerning reprimands being given to over a dozen employees for allegedly walking off the job. One of these employees happened to be my father. When an employee is given a reprimand, it is put in their record. An additional reprimand would result in suspension for a day, a third would result in a three day suspension and so on. The workers in this situation had not walked off the job, and they filed grievances when they were reprimanded. The Superintendent told me that if I withdrew the grievances of the other workers, he would see to it that the reprimand would not be added to my father's record. I told the Superintendent that there would be no way I would withdraw the grievances of these other workers regardless of his offer. It was not the fair thing to do and, once again, fairness is what the UAW was fighting for. The Superintendent thought he had an easy way out of this problem by attempting to manipulate me by using my father, but things would not be that easy for management as long as I was a committeeman. And I vowed they never would be.

To give some insight to how things worked within auto plants concerning union and management, I will explain the hierarchy in the GM plant in Marion where I was employed. There were five different departments in our plant: the shipping and receiving department where I worked, the metal assembly department, the press room, the tool and die department, and the maintenance department. Each of these five departments had a Superintendent who was in charge of the department and oversaw everything, a General Supervisor who ranked directly under the Superintendent, and at least one Supervisor (or Foreman) who was in charge of the workers. And, of course, each department had a Union Committeeman like myself. The workers came to me, and then I would speak to the Foreman, then the General Supervisor, and then the Superintendent. When I had official meetings with the Superintendent, I would be accompanied by a Union Chairman or another committeeman. The Superintendent would be accompanied by a member of labor relations. Labor relations was part of management and they dealt with all employee records and were involved an all grievances.

John H. Jackson

Grievance Procedure

One of the most essential rights of UAW members is to resolve problems with management through the negotiated grievance procedure. The grievance procedure varies from plant to plant, but the basic steps are similar. When a union member has a complaint with his or her supervisor, he or she will first try to settle it with the supervisor. If the complaint cannot be settled with the supervisor, the employee has the right to request union representation. At this point, a call is put in for the Committeeman. When a union member requests this call, the supervisor will make it with no delay and all discussion will then cease between the employee and the supervisor.

The Committeeman will then go to the employee to hear the complaint and investigate all the facts surrounding the problem. He then goes to the supervisor to discuss, and attempt to settle, the problem. If the problem cannot be settled between the supervisor and the union representative, the committeeman will then put the grievance in writing and take it to the General Supervisor. If the committeeman and the general supervisor cannot come to an agreement regarding the complaint, the next step is for the committeeman to go back to the employee and write an official grievance on the complaint. This grievance is given to the supervisor. At this time, the supervisor will either give an official reply to the grievance or he will sign the grievance and inform the committeeman that he will answer the grievance at a later date. Three copies are made of this signed grievance. The first copy is given to the supervisor, the second copy stays with union for the employee, and the third copy is for the committeeman's personal records.

There are different violations a committeeman may charge management with when writing a grievance. Thus, there are different ways of writing grievances. For example, if a committeeman is charging management with a violation of the National Agreement, the grievance would be written:

> *- The Union charges Management Supervisor John Doe with violation of Paragraph 215 of the National Agreement. I demand that said Supervisor be corrected of this violation immediately.*

The committeeman may also charge management with violation of the Local Agreement. This is an agreement negotiated by local management and the shop committee. This grievance would be written:

> *- The Union charges Management with violation of the local overtime agreement and Paragraph 71 of the National Agreement. The Union demands that said employee be paid all wages lost due to this violation.*

Another grievance is when a supervisor unjustly disciplines an employee. This grievance would be written:

> *- The Union charges Management Supervisor John Doe with unjustly giving said employee a reprimand. The Union demands that this*

reprimand be removed from said employee's
record immediately.

When the supervisor gives his answer on a grievance,
the committeeman will settle the grievance then or he will
send the grievance to the "one and a half step." That is
the department Superintendent. The committeemen will
set up a meeting with the Superintendent to attempt to
settle the grievance along with any other existing
grievances in the department. This could include
anywhere from five to seventy-five grievances, depending
on how much time had expired between meetings or how
much trouble we may have had since the last one and a
half step meeting.

Normally, we would have one meeting a week, but
there were times that we had two or three within a week.
At the one and half step meeting, I would be accompanied
by the Shop Committeeman or another union
representative. A member of labor relations would sit in
with the Superintendent. The grievances that we could
not settle during these meetings would move onto the
"second step."

At the second step meeting, labor relations and the
Shop Committee would attempt to settle the grievances.
The Shop Committee consisted of district committeemen
like myself who were elected to be on the Shop
Committee. Our plant in Marion had eleven district
committeemen, one for first and second shift in all five
districts within the plant and an eleventh committeemen
for all of the third shift. Every year (it is now every three
years) six of us were elected to the Shop Committee. This,
of course, followed the elections of the district
committeemen which were specific to each district. Once
the district elections were completed, there was a plant-

wide election to appoint the Shop Committee as well as the UAW Local President and the Chairman of the Shop Committee. The Chairman of the Shop Committee is the top union representative within the plant. He serves as the spokesperson for the Shop Committee and, within the plant, the local UAW.

There are usually second step meetings once a week where labor relations and the Shop Committee attempt to settle the unsettled grievances. Labor relations are accompanied by management and supervisors. The Chairman and the Shop Committee are accompanied by the UAW Local President who remains silent in the meetings. If grievances still cannot be settled, they move onto a "third step."

Once a grievance has reached the third step, the Chairman of the shop committee and the shop committeeman will write briefs on all of the unsettled grievances. The Chairman will then contact the UAW Region to notify them of the problems and request a regional representative be sent to the plant to assist the Chairman in the third step. UAW Regions are larger factions of the National Union set up to help the smaller local unions, and regional representatives are elected nationally. At the third step meeting, the Chairman of the shop committee, accompanied by the regional representative meets with the personnel director who is accompanied by a member of labor relations to attempt to settle the grievances. Even after the third step, some grievances will still remain unsettled. The chairman of the shop committee will write briefs on the unsettled grievances and send them to the "third and a half step."

In the third and a half step of the grievance procedure, the arbitration staff will take a look at the *grievance and attempt to settle it before sending it to the arbitrator. The arbitration staff is comprised of UAW members who, like the committeeman before them, study the grievances from all sides. There may be certain grievances that the union, for one reason or another, does not want the arbitrator to make a ruling on. The arbitration staff will find a way to settle these grievances before they come before the arbitrator. An arbitrator basically performs the duties of a judge. In fact, the men I knew who were employed as arbitrators were usually retired Judges who had served several years on Court benches. There would be a hearing for the grievance. The arbitrator would listen to both sides and then make a ruling. The arbitrator's salary is paid fifty percent by the union and fifty percent by General Motors and both parties have a say in the hiring process to ensure the impartiality of the arbitrator.*

I had the opportunity to sit in on an arbitrator meeting regarding one of my grievances as committeeman. It was a discharge case and the arbitrator ruled against the union. Although we lost the ruling in that particular grievance, I felt the arbitrator meeting to be fair and professional.

The grievance procedure is just another way that union and management can solve problems by negotiating rather than resulting to violence. It gives workers a chance to speak up and be heard, and also be represented by a committeeman sympathetic to their situation. The grievance procedure of the UAW and General Motors prevents strikes and violence and it is one of the vital, necessary attributes to the progress between union and management.

Chapter Four

During the first few years of the sixties, my first years as committeeman, supervision and higher management tried in any and every way they could to change me. They hoped to get me to do things their way and to look the other way concerning the problems they were causing in the plant, but I was a union man and I had already begun to realize the true importance of that, as well as the responsibility that came with being a union representative.

In 1963, I attended a meeting in Detroit where I was privileged enough to see and hear Walter Ruether speak. This was one of the most inspirational moments of my life. Reuther was a tremendous speaker. He knew, better than anyone I had ever seen, how to passionately convey a message and get his point across in a way that everyone could understand. I knew, at this point, that my heart and soul were dedicated to the union and its causes. In 1965, at another meeting, I had the amazing opportunity to meet Walter Reuther. Not only is he one of, if not the, greatest union leaders in American history, but Walter Reuther was an enthusiastic man who truly cared about the union movement as well as the Civil Rights Movement. He had dedicated his life to those causes and he would talk to you about civil rights and the union for as long as you would care to talk. His obvious and intense conviction inspired me greatly, and I would carry this inspiration with me for the next thirty-five years, working as a union man.

In the mid 1960s, American liberalism hit its high water mark. President Lyndon B. Johnson, who took office after the assassination of John F. Kennedy, got Congress to pass the Civil Rights Act in 1964. In 1965, the Voting Rights Act was made law. Johnson had announced a war on poverty, among other things, as part of his goal of what he termed "the Great Society."

Labor unions thrived in the sixties, as the nation's successful economy relied on a sizeable manufacturing industry to maintain its growth. The Civil Rights Act of 1964 made a very important contribution to national labor policy. The Civil Rights Act declared it an unfair labor practice for an employer, or union, to discriminate against a person by reason of race, sex, religion, color, or national origin. Administration of this declaration is vested in the Equal Employment Opportunities Commission. Under the Civil Rights Act, if the EEOC is unable to achieve compliance, the person alleging discrimination is then authorized to bring a civil action to federal court. All of this had an overwhelming effect within the automobile industry and its unions in that any unions that had maintained an all-white membership would now be desegregated. Working conditions for blacks, women, and migrant workers were improved considerably. For the UAW and its president Walter Reuther, things were definitely headed in the right direction.

Reuther had always seen the pure connection between the labor movement and the Civil Rights Movement. He had fought for the basic rights of auto workers, improving the pay and working conditions for all workers, making sure that even unskilled workers were included, taken care of by the union, and not taken advantage of by management. As the sixties continued and the Civil

Rights Movement forced itself into the nation's consciousness, Reuther got behind the movement in every way that he could. He backed Dr. Martin Luther King and funded the organizations that would spawn the New Left. The Student Nonviolent Coordinating Committee (SNCC) and the Congress of Racial Equality (CORE) which spearheaded Freedom Summer in Mississippi were funded by Reuther. He also funded Students for a Democratic Society (SDS). Reuther not only understood the importance of the fight for civil rights and its relation to the union movement, but he saw hypocrisy in not linking the two movements. He fought for the lives of all workers, not just white males. Reuther attacked those labor unions with an all-white membership. While other union leaders, like George Meaney, the head of the AFL-CIO, had turned their backs on fighting discrimination in the plants and in the unions, Reuther made it his top priority.

Walter Reuther did not stop there. In the late sixties, he began to see another of his ambitious visions come to fruition. The UAW began the construction of a family education center located in the northern woods of Michigan at Black Lake. Reuther had envisioned Black Lake as a place that union members could bring their families to vacation, relax, and learn at the same time. With the help of his wife May, he began laying the blueprint in the early sixties. As president of the UAW, he worked hard to fund the project which had become a shared dream of both he and his wife. The Reuthers spent the majority of their time in the late sixties at Black Lake, overseeing the construction of their dream. UAW members had started to visit the center even before its completion, and Reuther told all visitors that his vision was "about the most critical issue of our times: the quality of leadership...The great changes taking place around us are straining the fabric of the human community and we must find the leadership, at all levels, to solve the problems ahead - leaders who combine the technical competence with social vision, idealism, and commitment." Reuther spoke these words in 1970, shortly before a plane carrying him and his wife May from Black Lake to Detroit crashed, resulting in their untimely deaths. The education center was officially completed in 1974 and it was named the Walter and May Reuther Family Center. The Reuthers' dream became a real life experience that still thrives today. Families from all over the country and world visit Black Lake every year, taking advantage of the beautiful scenery and recreation facilities, and learning about the union and its importance.

All one has to do, as a union member, to visit Black Lake is fill out an application and declare what weeks you would like to go and then simply wait your turn. All expenses are paid by the UAW. In 1981, I had the opportunity to visit the Walter and May Reuther Family Center at Black Lake for a week. I could not believe my eyes when I arrived. It is a strikingly beautiful place where you can take your family, have fun and learn about the union at the same time. It is a large part of the enormous legacy that Walter Reuther left us. He was, without a doubt, the greatest union leader that ever lived.

The death of UAW President Walter Reuther shocked the automobile industry. It was a devastating blow to the union, for Reuther was not only the president of the UAW, he was the most recognizable and charismatic union leader of his time. Reuther had transcended the industrial union movement. Even considering all he accomplished within the auto industry, his life and work had as much political and social influence on the country as it did industrial and economical. His death was a tremendous loss, but his fight and his accomplishments will forever live.

Leonard Woodcock stepped into to fill the big shoes of Reuther, becoming the UAW President in 1970. Not only was he replacing the most influential union leader of his time, Woodcock was now leading a very active union in an extraordinary time. Just two years earlier in 1968, the UAW left the AFL-CIO due in part to an argument over the UAW's distaste for the AFL-CIO's aggressive organizing of non-union workers and in larger part to the two organizations' difference of opinion concerning the war.

The United States was in the midst of the Vietnam War. Although many American history books refer to it as a "conflict," do not be fooled. 'Twas a war, and hundreds of thousands of innocent lives of all nationalities were being senselessly lost because of it. Walter Reuther and the UAW strongly opposed the war. In fact, several UAW locals had organized anti-war demonstrations as early as 1965.

The country had been divided into two simply defined sides concerning the Vietnam War, for or against. Leonard Woodcock would now be feeling the stress and pressure that Reuther had been dealing with, leading an organization that was opposed to the war within an industry that was looked to by the government during wartime. However, opposition to the Vietnam War was no surprise to the government. Not since the Civil War, had our country been so obviously divided.

In 1968, both Dr. Martin Luther King, Jr. and Robert Kennedy were assassinated. King was the most important and influential figure in the Civil Rights Movement, and both he and Kennedy were supporters of the union. There was no doubt that the New Left was under attack. The dinosaurs still holding a great deal of control throughout the government and industry, who based their lives and careers on the racist ideals of the old south and other outdated and ignorant philosophies, felt extremely threatened by the movement taking place in the U.S. at this time. Citizens who clung to these ideals also felt threatened. There was a new generation who were educated, passionate, undyingly opposed to the war, and not only ready for change, but ready to make change happen. A unifying effort began to take place in the United States, centered around opposition to the war, but also including the Civil Rights Movement as well as the union movement, and, as Bob Dylan sang in a popular song of the time, the times they were a changin'.

After Lyndon B. Johnson's presidency came to an end in 1968, Richard Nixon took office as the President of the United States at the beginning of 1969. He would be the leader of a country at war, a war that a majority of the country's citizens did not support. Political and social organizations had been formed all over the nation, and these groups would protest, demonstrate, and literally fight for the rights of African-Americans, women, as well as the working man. These were turbulent times in America.

Fortunately, the UAW had chosen a brilliant man for its president in Leonard Woodcock. Woodcock shared Reuther's general philosophy that the mission of the labor movement should strive for human rights and social justice along with economical justice for all working Americans. Woodcock would not have to wait to showcase his beliefs or to prove to the union his amazing skills as a negotiator. Just months after taking office as UAW President in 1970, Woodcock led UAW members in a historic strike against the General Motors Corporation.

John H. Jackson

1970 Strike against General Motors

Other than a minor ten day shutdown in 1964, the UAW had not struck against General Motors since 1946, but long-simmering resentments between the union and the corporation came to the forefront in 1970 and became headline news. An increasing number of demands were being made by UAW locals regarding a number of growing concerns, the majority concerning health, safety, and other working conditions.

The UAW International Convention in April 1970 had given the Union's Bargaining Committee a substantial list of issues to take to the bargaining table. The bargaining process was expected to long and arduous. Adding to the anxiety of local leaders, it was becoming clear that the strike target for this round of international negotiations would be General Motors. It was standard operating procedure for a strike target to be selected by the International union one or two weeks before the strike deadline. If no contracts were agreed to by the deadline, then only the target would be struck. This brought anxiety because GM had always been the toughest corporation to take on. UAW leaders knew that if GM was the target, the strike would be a long one. The strike of 1945-46 had lasted one hundred thirteen days.

Experience had already proven that once an agreement was reached with the target corporation, settlements with the remaining auto companies came easy, due to the fact that those companies could be assured that labor costs would remain equal across the automobile industry. This would allow auto companies to remain competitive.

By July 1970, negotiations were set to begin on the national and local levels. The stakes were high for the International union. The outcome of these negotiations would affect the future of 713,000 workers throughout the industry, 395,000 at General Motors, alone. Wages were among the major issues. Under the old contract, the average auto worker made $4.02 an hour. The UAW wanted a sixty-three cent an hour raise in pay. GM offered thirty-eight cents. Another issue was the old contract's eight cent an hour cap on cost of living raises. The UAW had fought for and won cost of living raises in 1948. The cost of living was now increasing at a much more rapid pace, and an eight cent an hour cap seemed ridiculous and unfair. Union members also sought a "thirty and out" provision which would provide monthly pensions of five hundred dollars to workers with thirty years of service.

Negotiations continued into September with GM, Chrysler, and Ford. No progress had been made at Ford or GM. UAW President Woodcock announced, a week before the strike deadline, that Chrysler would not be the strike target because he had learned that GM leaders had pressured Chrysler to turn away from a near settlement. With the UAW announcement two weeks earlier that Ford would not be the strike target, as anticipated, General Motors would be the target for the strike.

It appeared as though General Motors was eager to take on the union. Earl Bramblett, GM Vice President in charge of personnel and the chief negotiator for the corporation, stated that the UAW's refusal to accept GM's offer would result in a "strike against reason." A statement such as this only strengthened union leaders' resentment toward the corporation. The UAW knew how unreasonable Bramblett and GM had been with their offers in response to all of the union demands, and, at this point, there were even more eager to strike.

The UAW notified its members that the strike deadline was set for midnight on Monday September 14th. Both sides, GM and the UAW, acknowledged that negotiators were "far apart." Local negotiators were also reporting no progress. So, as the clock struck twelve on the morning of September 14, 1970, the walkout began, and it went without incident. Pickets went up immediately at one hundred fifty-five locals across the United States and Canada. Twenty-seven GM parts plants were not struck to allow production to continue of parts that were to be sold to Chrysler and Ford. GM's Bramblett commented on the walkout, "the UAW always starts out with fantastic demands and this year the demands are more fantastic...I very honestly did not expect a strike this year." For union leaders and members, these were curious comments considering they were coming from a man who himself seemed anxious for a battle with the UAW, and who was representing a corporation that appeared equally anxious and prepared for a strike. UAW President Woodcock felt that GM actively sought a strike and he stated, "We had no ideological problems...it was simply a matter of arithmetic. I believe the reason they have taken this hard line is that they have other fish to fry."

The UAW knew it was in for a long strike. The International strike fund was at one hundred twenty million dollars. Each union member with a family was allotted forty dollars a week in strike pay. Union leaders figured that the strike fund would last seven to eight weeks. There was a great deal of apprehension among the union as to whether that would be long enough.

The General Motors Corporation called in labor relations chiefs from all of its divisions on September 19th, as the company began to realize the urgent need to break stalemates and begin serious negotiations on the local level. Woodcock had made it known that the local-level working agreements, which supplemented the national wage package, must be completed in all one hundred fifty-five locations before any of the hundreds of thousands of workers would return to their jobs. This was a daring ultimatum put forth by Woodcock. In past strikes, local negotiations often continued for weeks after a national settlement was reached. Now, all thirty thousand local demands would have to be settled before any plants would be allowed to start up. This was a risky, hard-nosed move by the UAW president and it added to the union's anxiety concerning the strike fund, but it was daring moves like this one that made Leonard Woodcock famous for his skills as a negotiator.

A special Constitutional Convention was held in Detroit on October 2nd to address the strike insurance program. President Woodcock informed representatives from the UAW locals that a National Committee had been formed with the sole purpose of aiding UAW members and families of UAW members who were striking against General Motors. The Committee was headed by former Illinois Senator Paul Douglas and included such people as Hubert Humphrey, Ted Kennedy, and Mrs. Martin Luther King, Jr. among others. Woodcock stated at the Convention, "I want to commend the entire membership of the UAW on the solidarity displayed throughout this period of time. We know that these are not the most favorable conditions, but we need your continued support until we do have a fair and equitable agreement that w can live with for years to come, both at the local and national levels."

The grueling strike continued. On November 3rd, the UAW International called a special meeting of a General Motors conference to be held on November 12th and to be attended by the three hundred fifty GM delegates from locals across the nation. Speculation began to run high due to the fact that, as a rule, a conference was called only after a tentative agreement had been reached.

Bargaining had intensified. Since October 10th, negotiations were being conducted under a news blackout. The Union called on its twenty-five member International Executive Board to meet in Detroit on November 11th. With the Executive Board meeting on the 11th and the GM conference set for the 12th, negotiators held ten hour meetings on the 7th and 8th. In the past, night long bargaining sessions were an indication that a settlement was near. November 11th looked to be the deadline. At 2:00 a.m. on that day, after a seventeen hour bargaining session that broke only for meals, neither Woodcock nor GM's Bramblett would comment. The strike had been going for eight weeks, and both men were under tremendous pressure. It was feared that any more delay in reaching a settlement would push start up of GM production into December or even January. Both sides faced additional pressure with the threat of federal intervention. J. Curtis Count, director of the Federal Mediation and Conciliation Service, put the UAW and General Motors on Notice that the government would intervene to force a settlement if progress was not made soon.

Early on November 12th, an agreement was reached as the negotiating teams from the UAW and General Motors had finally settled national contract demands. These demands had been on the table for two months. There was now confidence that the 350,000 striking union members would be returning to work as their local contracts were settled. UAW President Woodcock said that he was "certain" that the UAW Executive Board and the GM Council would support all locals that could not reach agreement and wanted to continue striking.

Later, on the afternoon of the twelfth, the agreement was presented to GM Council and the strike was nearing its end. Contract provisions were kept from the media until they were approved by the Executive Board of the UAW and the GM Council. Some of the provisions in the new contract were:

- Wages will be adjusted to reflect the cost of living on a quarterly basis

- A wage increase of forty-nine to sixty-one cents an hour the first year of the contract

- Wage increases averaging twelve cents an hour for the second and third years

- Retirement pension of $500 a month after thirty years of service at age fifty-six

– Increase of $1.75 a month of basic pension payments for each year of service if retired at age sixty-five

- Four weeks of vacation pay after twenty years of service

John H. Jackson

Woodcock and the UAW had negotiated an amazingly beneficial and important new contract. Commenting on the contract, General Motors Vice-President Earl Bramblett called the settlement "inflationary." Once again, curious comments were coming from Bramblett considering that the General Motors Corporation was now a billion dollar company and could easily afford all the new contract provisions. And that was exactly the point the union was focusing on with the historic strike of 1970. The plant workers were putting all the muscle, time, and sweat that made the GM corporation and the auto industry run the way it did. With hundreds of millions of dollars coming into automobile corporations, it only seemed fair that the men and women who were doing the real work get a fair portion of the large profits they were earning for their companies.

I remember the year 1970 as if it were yesterday. It was an extremely sad year with the loss of our great leader and president, Walter Reuther. The deaths of he and his wife were a shocking blow for all of us in the UAW. The Executive Board met and elected Leonard Woodcock as our new president. This, of course, was a tragic time and it was also a contract year, but Woodcock stepped in with poise and confidence. I remember him saying that he would except the UAW presidency, but that there was no way he could fill the shoes of the great Walter Reuther.

As a union member, especially a committeeman, you always remember a contract year, and I certainly remember this one. We had faith in Woodcock. He had come up through the ranks behind Reuther and had learned a lot from him.

We all knew Woodcock was a great negotiator, and this was definitely what we needed for the new contract we sought.

In a contract year, negotiations on the local level usually begin months before the strike (contract) deadline. The UAW usually picks a strike target a couple of weeks before the deadline. We did not know who the strike target would be, but union members and representatives at my plant in Marion, Indiana, Local 977, felt that General Motors was going to be the strike target. We took a strike vote at Local 977 and it was passed by nearly 100%. If agreement had not been reached by the deadline, we would strike.

The strike began and it was a nervous and stressful time for all of us at GM and the UAW. It lasted sixty-seven days, but by its end, Woodcock's bargaining skills had lead to a landmark contract. I cannot say enough about the job he did for us in that strike. The new contract provided us with a number of much needed medical benefits such as prescription drugs and medical protection including hospital costs and surgery. The thirty and out provision was a big win for us. The entirety of the 1970 negotiations was a major victory for the UAW, and Leonard Woodcock had proved to be a great leader for the union.

As the early seventies continued, the landscape of politics and industry continued to change in the United States. The Watergate scandal came to light, and President Nixon was replaced by Gerald Ford in 1972. This, of course, exposed a frightening example of the corruption that was running through the government and corporate businesses in our country. The Nixon presidency had engaged in a number of practices, most of them illegal, to pick apart and destroy the New Left that had come to prominence with activists like Dr. Martin Luther King, Jr. and the UAW's Water Reuther. The UAW continued its fight for fairness within the automobile industry. Bargaining brought improved accident and sickness benefits in 1975 and paid personal holidays in 1976. Progress was still being made.

Chapter Five

In the 1970s, the volume of international trade spurted and American industries began to experience competition from foreign imports. Automobiles were the major factor in the acceleration of import growth. While this was happening, the UAW was having trouble with the sub-contracting taking place at the General Motors Corporation. The corporation was sending auto parts work to other countries where the parts were made and then shipped back to this country to be assembled. The majority of this work was going to Mexico where the big American corporations could send their work to be done much cheaper and without union interference. While this was happening, American auto workers were being laid off at a swift pace.

We were experiencing a lot of problems in my plant in Marion, Indiana due to the sub-contracting. In fact, it was, by far, the biggest problem we were dealing with during the seventies. All of us at the UAW Local 977 were fighting hard against what we saw as a travesty. General Motors advertised an American made product, but their parts were being made in another country. Of course, it came down to money. GM was well aware of how little they could pay Mexican workers to do their labor. They also knew they could do this and steer clear of the union. I will not even begin to get into the morality of it all. It was wrong, and the saddest thing is that this is something that the UAW still has to fight against, close to thirty years later.

81

The recession of 1974 and 1975 had stalled industry growth and had made life hard on American working men and women. In 1976, Democrat Jimmy Carter was elected to replace Republican Gerald Ford as the President of the United States. The union, as well as the working class, always benefits from having a democrat in office. UAW President Leonard Woodcock, a dedicated political activist, had rallied his million member union to support the Carter campaign. Woodcock's efforts did not go unnoticed. When Woodcock stepped down from the UAW Presidency in 1977, at age sixty-five, President Carter asked him to lead a mission to Vietnam and Laos to retrieve the remains of twelve American servicemen. These were extremely delicate negotiations, yet Woodcock was successful. This mission not only ended with Woodcock's return to the United States with the remains of the twelve servicemen, it had established the groundwork for normal relations between the United States and both Vietnam and Laos. This was yet another example of a union leader making the transition to politics and government and not only having success, but truly making a difference. Carter rewarded Woodcock with the post of U.S. liaison to China. In 1979, Woodcock became the United States' first Ambassador to the People's Republic of China. The union was producing more than automobiles and better lives for auto workers. The union was producing important leaders for and of this nation.

Woodcock's mission to Vietnam and Laos also served as an example of President Carter's focus on foreign relations. This was his biggest success as President of the United States. In fact, he still continues to contribute his skills in foreign relations to our government twenty-five years after his presidency. In 1979, Carter and his administration, including Leonard Woodcock, negotiated one of the most significant diplomatic agreements of our time when they were able to normalize trade relations between the United States and China. The majority of UAW members opposed the normalization between the two countries. Woodcock addressed this by stating, "I have been startled by organized labor's vociferous negative reaction to this agreement. The reality is that the U.S. as a whole benefits mightily from this historic accord. Democracy is an evolutionary process. Isolation and containment will not promote improved rights for a people. Rather, working together and from within a society will, over time, promote improved conditions. The U.S.-China WTO agreement will speed up the evolutionary process in China. American labor should support it."

Leonard Woodcock, like Walter Reuther and other union leaders before him, focused on the big picture. He knew that having normal rather than abnormal relations with China would put American industry in a position to maximize its exports. At the same time, it would maximize the United States' ability to enhance the cause of freedom in China. Woodcock was able to look beyond business and yet, keep a strong focus on what would have a positive effect on both industry and the working man. The agreement with China included several clearly positive aspects for the U.S.:

1) The United States gives no tariff reductions or additional market entry whatsoever. China lowers its tariffs drastically and open its markets. (the U.S. gives nothing, China gives everything.)

2) The U.S. can now stop surges of Chinese exports. It could not before. (these were the strongest anti-surge laws ever legislated)

3)   The U.S. negotiated a provision that enabled our country to stop imports from slave and prison labor.

Once again, going beyond business, this agreement also maximized the United States' influence over any future tensions that might occur between China and other countries such as India, South Korea, Taiwan, and Japan. It was a clear victory for the Carter Administration and Leonard Woodcock. It was progress.

In the automobile industry during the late seventies, relations with foreign countries would prove to be a serious issue. Auto companies began to sub-contract work to Mexico which resulted in American workers losing jobs. The UAW was in an uproar. There were issues of child labor practices in Mexico at the time. This and the fact that American auto companies prided themselves on an American made product, especially with the growth in imports, was simply unethical. The union fought hard against the sub-contracting with little success.

The auto companies were in an uproar of their own, concerned with the increasing number of imported automobiles coming into the U.S. American corporations were having a tough time adjusting to the new competition. Importing of oil and U.S. relations with the countries involved with this importing would also become a major concern for the automobile industry as the price of gasoline began to rise.

In the early seventies, the automobile industry was booming. The big three automakers, Ford, Chrysler, and General Motors, held what was basically a monopoly on the American market. Up to this point, cars imported from foreign countries had yet to make much of an impact on the automobile industry in the United States. This meant extremely large profits for American corporations. Over the course of the late seventies and early eighties, this would change drastically.

Recession hit the country in 1974 and 1975. Policy makers perceived inflation as the major problem. To explain a complex situation simply, the Federal Reserve instilled a tighter monetary policy which produced higher interest rates which, in turn, reduced the level of investment purchases. The decline in investment purchases resulted in a decline in production. This resulted in a higher unemployment rate. This was the intention of the Federal Reserve's tighter monetary policy for it believed that higher unemployment and a decline in production would discourage price increases. However, recession did not have the intended effect on inflation and the unemployment rate grew close to ten percent. The government worried that the American public would start talking depression rather than recession. The Ford Administration and Congress sought an anti-recession policy in hopes to stimulate the economy, but the damage had been done.

Of course, as history proves, any downturn in the American economy tends to affect the middle class more than anyone else. The middle class is the working class, and these working men and women were dealing with unemployment, less pay, and higher prices. Included in these higher prices was the skyrocketing price of gasoline. This affected the American automobile industry in an enormous way. When gas prices were nearly doubled in 1979 and 1980, the demand for the larger American made cars was greatly reduced, and the demand for the smaller cars produced by foreign manufacturers increased rapidly. The middle class Americans that had been the core customers for companies like General Motors and Ford were now buying from foreign companies, combating the higher gas prices by driving smaller cars with better gas mileage.

The percent of imported automobiles rose from 17.7% in 1978 to 21.8% in 1979 and 26.7% in 1980. The majority of the increase in imports came from Japan, so the U.S. automobile industry sought to limit Japan's imports by having Japan auto manufacturers sign a "voluntary" agreement to reduce them, providing the rationale that the agreement was necessary to aid the U.S. auto industry in adjusting to sharply changed circumstances and consumer preferences and explaining that the U.S. automobile industry was an industry that needed time and massive investment to fully adjust to these new circumstances. An agreement was signed with Japan in 1981 that would result in an eight percent reduction of their automobile imports. This agreement gave the U.S. industry time to focus on the production of more economical vehicles and withstand the competition from foreign markets.

While the government and corporations concentrated on business relations with other countries, we at the UAW Locals continued to focus on making progress and bettering the lives of the working class. As time passed and I continued to serve as shop committeeman and district committeeman at my plant in Marion, Indiana, I began to see some progress being made between management and the union. Some trust seemed to be developing between supervisors and committeemen. In the past, it was commonplace for a supervisor to go through labor relations to deal with a problem concerning an employee. Now, more and more, the supervisor was calling me and he and I would deal with the problem with the employee. This was saving time and hassle and it was strengthening the relationship between union and management. This was incredibly important. Both sides were well aware of the inevitable tension that would exist between us due to the simple fact that we were on opposite sides, but we were beginning to see the promise in dealing with one another with sophistication and decency rather than with quick tempers and hostility.

In the late seventies and early eighties, the UAW focused strongly on several aspects of health and safety conditions within automobile factories. We sought to set up joint programs with General Motors to benefit employees, better the workplace, and, in turn, better the product we were producing. Of course, these joint programs would take serious cooperation between union and management, not to mention a fair share of negotiating and bargaining to set up the programs, but I believe we had all begun to notice the progress that was being made regarding the relationship between workers and management as well as the evolution of attitudes that had taken place. We were ready to start addressing, together, the things that would improve all aspects of the industry and the lives of its workers. While we at the Local 977, and the men and women at UAW Locals all over the country, began digging into these issues, our new UAW President Douglas Fraser was handling national issues that would prove to be monumental.

Douglas Fraser worked his way up through the ranks to become the sixth president of the United Automobile Workers in 1977 when Leonard Woodcock reached the age of sixty-five and stepped down. Fraser had served beside Woodcock after being elected Vice-President of the UAW in 1970. He worked with Walter Reuther in 1964, leading the UAW bargaining committee at Chrysler where the union had secured its historic early retirement program. He again led negotiations at the Chrysler Corporation in 1967, and he won the first wage parity agreement between the United States and Canada. After a successful nine day strike in 1973, Fraser, along with Woodcock, again lead the negotiations at Chrysler. This particular bargaining resulted in a number of contract gains including accelerated arbitration, an improved thirty and out early retirement plan, restrictions on compulsory overtime, and a comprehensive health and safety program.

The biggest challenge for Fraser during his tenure as UAW President came in 1979. The Chrysler Corporation was dangerously close to bankruptcy. If the corporation went bankrupt, it would mean that over one hundred thousand men and women, union members, would lose their jobs. This would be a disaster to say the least, and it was about to happen. Then Doug Fraser stepped up and, along with Michigan Senator Donald Riegle and Congressman James Blanchard, he went to President Jimmy Carter and Congress to lobby for a federal loan...and literally save the Chrysler Corporation.

Saving Chrysler was undoubtedly Fraser's biggest fight, but as he himself would point out, it was also the UAW's biggest crisis. The union faced an enormous amount of lost jobs, but Fraser's lobbying was successful. He, Riegle, and Blanchard received $1.5 billion in federal loan guarantees for Chrysler from Carter and Congress. This was huge. It saved Chrysler. Fraser immediately negotiated new contracts with the corporation and saved 140,000 union jobs.

Another of Fraser's accomplishments during these dealings with the Chrysler Corporation was a pure example of the progress that was being made between company management and the UAW. Fraser persuaded union workers to grant benefit and wage concessions to Chrysler three times within fourteen months. This showed the compassion workers had for their company's situation as well as their loyalty to their UAW President.

Fraser's efforts were rewarded by the Chrysler Corporation when he was named a member of the Executive Board of Directors at Chrysler in 1980. This was a groundbreaking accomplishment for Fraser and the UAW. Never before had a union leader become an executive member of an automobile corporation. Walter Reuther and Leonard Woodcock had played significant roles within politics and government, and now Fraser had secured an important and influential position within the business side of the auto industry. The union and its leaders continued to progress to heights that forty years earlier would have seemed unreachable. These were working class men from working class families who had struggled, fighting their way through the ranks - fighting against the ranks to better the lives of their fellow workers. Now, these working class men were becoming executives and government officials. That is progress.

Just months before being named to the Board at Chrysler, Fraser led the 1979 round of negotiations for the first time as President of the UAW. He pushed for, and successfully obtained for the union, frequent increases in pension benefits for retirees, both current and future. He also secured improvements in the cost of living allowances formula as well as reduced work time.

In 1982, a two hundred five day strike at Caterpillar, Inc. ended in victory for the UAW. Fraser and the union successfully fought off corporate demands for concessions. President Fraser had picked up where Leonard Woodcock had left off, leading the union to improved contracts and better lives. His spot on the Board of Chrysler, alone, was monumental in that it gave the union a voice within the management of a corporation for the first time.

Douglas Fraser retired from the UAW in 1983 and became a distinguished and respected professor of labor studies. He continues to teach and lecture, telling stories of the racial and sexual discrimination he witnessed workers go through in the automobile industry and, as he says, giving "a broad view of society, the ills of society and the disproportionate distribution of wealth." Before, during, and after his time as UAW President, Douglas Fraser had not only directly influenced the progress of the working men and women within the automobile industry, he stood as one of the strongest examples of how truly influential union men and women could be in business and politics as well as in the fight for labor rights.

Chapter Six

The 1980s was a decade of struggle for the automobile industry as well as for working men and women, in general. Ronald Reagan had become President of the United States in 1980, and, within two years, the country was experiencing another recession. This was the worst recession this nation had seen since the Great Depression. By 1982, the unemployment rate was 9.7%. That is dangerously high. I felt fortunate to be working in the auto industry during this time. The union had spent decades securing its workers welfare, especially for times like these. That is not to say auto workers were not losing there jobs during the eighties because they most certainly were, but, solely because of the UAW and its successes, we had a great deal more job and wage security than workers in other areas of employment. Even in the midst of the anti-labor, anti-union climate created by Reagan and his Vice-President George Bush, we at the UAW continued to fight for improvement.

Our new UAW President, Owen Bieber, took office in 1983. He was another great negotiator for the union. Beiber concentrated on protecting our jobs and our pay in the horrible economic times of the eighties. He also continued the fight for progress that Doug Fraser had started regarding extreme improvement concerning health and safety in auto plants. Bieber, like Fraser, not only sought to better the working conditions within the factories, he sought to educate workers and management by setting up an international program focusing on health and safety in the automobile industry. As I will address later in this chapter, this health and safety

91

program would directly affect my career as a union man and as a worker for General Motors.

When Owen Bieber assumed the UAW presidency in 1983, he entered into difficult times for industry and the economy. We were in the midst of a recession that was presenting itself in the usual ways of unemployment and poverty, but now the country was seeing a new, overwhelming problem in homelessness. The economy had reached a treacherously low point under the Reagan Administration where men and women were falling into to debt so far and so fast that they were losing their homes. This problem only escalated throughout the eighties.

President Reagan's economic plan, "Reaganomics," had begun to expose itself. The plan was widening the gap and adding to the struggle between the capitalist class and the working class. In the history of the United States, the distribution of wealth had never been so unbalanced. The rich were getting richer and the poor weren't only getting poorer, they were losing their jobs and homes. They were starving.

Just as we are experiencing today, in 2003, the President and his administration focused on the National Defense, pouring billions of dollars into the production of war goods, rather than focusing that money on the obvious problems that U.S. citizens were experiencing right here at home. The national deficit grew with Reagan's presidency. Jobs were being lost at a rapid rate and industry was struggling.

This was the climate that Owen Bieber entered into as the new UAW President. His focus would be to aggressively protect union members' jobs and wages. Reagan was simply destroying the economy, and he and his administration were against unionism. That is why former UAW President Fraser and his union fought hard to combat Reagan's campaign in 1980. The UAW could foresee the damage that would be done by the republican Reagan. Now, the damage was definitely being done. Bieber and the UAW would fight an uphill battle in their struggle to prevent Reagan's reelection in 1984 (to no avail) because it was apparent that the working class and the union were in desperate need of a democrat in office.

One solid example of this need concerned the federal loan Doug Fraser had secured for the Chrysler Corporation with the help of the democratic Carter Administration. Once this loan came under the guise of the republican Reagan Administration, the magnitude of this deal started to surface. Positively, the loan had saved Chrysler, and when Fraser's hard work was rewarded with a spot on the Executive Board at Chrysler it was a huge step for the union. Negatively, however, a problem arose in that the auto industry was now entering into a stage of government intervention and control. With Carter, the relationship between government and industry was, at least, fair. Now, with the capitalistic Reagan Administration, an important part of the contract between Chrysler and the government was coming back to bite the union.

Walter Reuther once said, "Free labor and free management working together can coexist and negotiate fair labor agreements without the intervention or the need of the government." This was all changing. When Chrysler agreed to accept the loan guarantee from the U.S. government, it transferred its fundamental powers to the government. This means that the corporation cannot take any steps without the approval of the government, not even simple tasks such as providing maintenance or office supplies.

The implications this had on the union were that the Chrysler division of the UAW was no longer negotiating with an individual company. It was now dealing with the collective strength of the nation's ruling class, a ruling class that was quickly becoming an unsympathetic, capitalist monster. The union's relationship with Chrysler changed tremendously now that the corporation had become, reluctantly, somewhat of an agent of the U.S. government, thrusting the union into a direct struggle, not just with the Chrysler Corporation, and not just with individuals on the Loan Board. The union was now in direct struggle against the capitalist state.

Just as the union had battled management for years, management and the union, together, now struggled against the government. The struggle of industry and union against the capitalist government is undoubtedly a book in and of itself, so let us focus on the progress that had been made, and began to show itself, at this time.

By the 1980s, the UAW had built a unique relationship with the executives of the largest corporations in the automobile industry. Because of the power of the UAW, the heads of corporations such as General Motors and Ford had grown anxious over the years to establish a strong, personal relationship with the strong union. Company heads and union men became accustomed to meeting with each other privately, dealing with each other on an equal level with respect, and even forming friendships. This was a far cry from the violence and struggle of the 1930s.

In the 1980s, the progress that had been made between union and management became even more evident. When I became a union committeeman in the late fifties, union men and management were at odds, to say the least. There wasn't a lot of respect being passed around. As the years went by, I think that both sides began to see the importance and the benefit in working together. Even though we were on completely different sides of most issues, there was no valid reason that we couldn't deal with each other with a certain level of respect. Once Reagan and Bush came into office, the union and the corporations started to realize that we did have some things in common. We were pitted together against the capitalist state created by the republican administrations. It was at this time that one could truly start to see the difference in the way we were dealing with one another. We were actually dealing with one another on a first name basis, even becoming friendly in some instances. If you had told me, twenty years prior, that this would be happening, I would have labeled you crazy. This was growth. This was progress.

The new UAW President Bieber took office in troubling, and even hostile, times for industry. As he concentrated on job and wage security, he and the union also ambitiously sought to create a number of joint programs between corporations and the union to better the worklife of auto employees.

Former UAW President Fraser had begun to address ideas for joint programs at the big three automobile corporations before Beiber took over. When Beiber did takeover, he aggressively focused on these joint programs, making his belief known that improvements in the workplace and in the lives of workers would lead to an increase in production as well as a better product.

By the mid 1980s, joint programs had been started at plants all over the automobile industry. These programs included health and safety committees, training programs, quality of worklife programs, and programs designed to help employees with drug and alcohol problems. The joint programs made an impact immediately. Production output increased as did the quality of the product. Most importantly, these joint programs contributed enormously to the progress being made between the union and management. All of the programs were structured so that union men and women were working, not only alongside, but with management and supervisors, compromising and sharing ideas. Walter Reuther's vision of a society where the working class could find job security and a fair living wage had come to fruition; not to say it was not something that the UAW still fought to maintain, especially during the reign of Reagan and Bush. However, the progress resulting in union and management working side by side, helping one another, addressing one another on a first name basis, and even becoming friends was, more than likely, not even foreseen by Reuther himself, a man of remarkable vision and optimism. With a quick look back to the bloody violence and intense struggle that transpired simply because auto workers were attempting to organize, the progress that had been made was nothing short of amazing.

Over the course of my 38 and a half years at General Motors, the one thing I saw more than anything else was progress. That is the very thing that provided the inspiration for this book. When I began working for GM in

1956, I was well aware of the history of the union, the struggle and the violence that had taken place twenty years earlier. I entered into an environment that might have been a little less bloody, but it was not any less hostile. When I started serving as a union committeeman, I truly became aware of the battle line between union and management. We were constantly at odds. From grievances to collective bargaining, we fought each other. We may have been working together in theory, but we were on opposite sides of the table, and there was definitely no love lost between those two sides.

As time went on, especially during the seventies and eighties, I started to see the line between the two sides begin to blur a bit, in a positive way for everyone. Having to deal with one another consistently, it was inevitable that the men and women of the union and the men and women of the company (executives, management, supervisors) would get to know one another, on a work basis at least. We were now getting to know one another personally, beginning to realize that we were all just people regardless of our job titles. I do not mean to paint it euphoric because it was far from it, but positive change was taking place. The joint programs were giving everyone the chance to witness the benefits that could come from working together, listening to one another, and compromising for the sake of both sides. The joint programs were also a testament to what a powerful entity the UAW had become.

All the joint programs the we started at General Motors were positive and beneficial. I felt that one of the best programs was the drug and alcohol program. If an employee had a problem with drugs and/or alcohol, he or she was able to go and see a union representative in a private office, behind closed doors. They would discuss

97

the problem in a completely confidential way. No one on the production floor would know about it. The union representative assigned to this program would work with the member of management who had been assigned to the program. They would work together to get the employee the proper help and care he or she was in need of. I saw this program change, and even save, lives. The corporation was finally recognizing drug and alcohol addiction as a disease. Up to this point, any worker who was struggling with addiction would be called to labor relations and laid off or simply fired. It made me sick because knew these men and women had problems. Losing their jobs certainly would not help matters, but finally these workers were being treated with compassion and provided with the attention they so desperately needed. This program really showed me the tremendous progress we had made with management. It also showed me that management was aware of the human condition; that the workers on these factory floors were not just robots or slaves. We were all human beings, union and management, and we were all in need of compassion and fairness.

By the mid 1980s, UAW membership was being negatively affected by the national recession as well as the large increase in imports and changing consumer preferences. In response, the UAW negotiated several joint programs with all three of the major auto corporations: Ford, Chrysler, and General Motors. The innovative joint programs addressed job and income security as well as a variety of concerns related to the workplace such as education and training, quality, family needs, and health and safety.

With the challenging political climate and the horrible state of the economy, it was ingenious for the UAW and the auto corporations to turn their focus on the workforce and the individual plants. They developed programs that would serve both sides well, improving the economic standing of workers while, at the same time, addressing company concerns about efficiency and productivity. Simply put, a safe and well trained worker with a secure job results in better work and a better product. It made perfect sense for the major corporations to adhere to the UAW's ideas, and it benefited union men and women greatly. These programs also created several new jobs for UAW members within the International Union, including serving as teachers and trainers to supervisors and management. How far the union had come.

John H. Jackson

Serving as a Health and Safety Instructor for the UAW

On November 29, 1988, I was assigned to the International UAW to become a health and safety instructor for committeeman and supervisors in training. This health and safety program was negotiated in the mid 1980s, and when it was made known that there would be a job opening as an instructor for the International Union, I immediately applied for the job. I knew this would be a great opportunity for me to delve even deeper into the union. I would be teaching, but I would also be learning, as well as traveling and meeting union members and General Motors supervisors from all over the United States.

Before starting the health and safety program, we went through a six week training program on how to become effective and successful health and safety instructors. We were given several pointers concerning public speaking such as controlling nerves and using proper vocal inflection. And, of course, we were trained extensively on all of the health and safety issues that workers were dealing with in GM plants. We outlined our teaching agenda and prepared to share our knowledge with all of the supervisors and union members that would be traveling to learn.

As instructors, we were assigned to different regional areas throughout the country. I was assigned to St. Louis,

Missouri. There were three other instructors assigned to St. Louis with me, two of which were GM supervisors and one who was a union representative like myself. The four instructors were divided into two teams, each compromised of one union representative and one supervisor.

Each week, we were to train forty people, twenty union committeeman and twenty supervisors. Of course, this meant that a supervisor and a union rep. would be working together, side by side, teaching other supervisors and union members who would be learning together, side by side. I would say that it was this experience, more than any other, that inspired the title of this book to be "Progress." The other union representative and I already had our tight common bond and we knew we would get along splendidly, but, as it turned out, the two GM supervisors that I worked alongside, one from Youngstown, Ohio and one from Tuscaloosa, Alabama, were two of the finest people I ever had the chance to work with. The progress we were making went beyond simply working together, we were getting to know each other personally and becoming friends. This was all pretty surreal. When I began work at General Motors thirty years prior to this, if someone would have told me that a union man and a company man would be working together, let alone becoming friendly, I would have not hesitated to call them crazy. But this was actually happening and we were making progress.

The progress was not limited to the instructors. Every week, twenty different union committeeman and twenty different GM supervisors would come to class, and as they learned together, they too came to know one another personally and became friendly as well.

John H. Jackson

We held our class at the Sheraton Hotel in St. Louis. It was a beautiful place that provided both an elegant and relaxed atmosphere for our program. The staff treated us with the utmost attention and respect, and our accommodations were more than satisfactory. All four instructors were given huge, executive suites to live in, and I honestly felt like a king. To have come from my less than humble upbringing in the hills of Kentucky to traveling, staying in luxurious hotels, and serving my union as a representative and a health and safety instructor allowed me to truly recognize the progress I had made as a man, along with the progress we were making as an industry. The union and the corporations were finally working together more than against one another. And the twenty GM supervisors and twenty union committeemen that would travel to St. Louis for these classes each week would stay together on the floor that the Sheraton had reserved for our class members, living side by side, eating together, and congregating in the evening to have fun and blow off steam together. Every Monday night, at the beginning of the week of classes, all forty-four of us would get together in the banquet room for our weekly party, full of drinks and eats. This allowed us to become acquainted with one another in a loose setting. All of these men and women, supervisors and union representatives, would push aside any turmoil or animosity they had regarding work, grievances, and the like, and share in a celebratory atmosphere with one another. It was a beautiful, and sometimes unbelievable sight.

All of this made me proud to be part of the health and safety program. I was able to witness, not only the progress that had been made up to this point, but also the progress we were making within this very program. I am still extremely proud of what we accomplished with the health and safety program. We came together to become educated about the safety issues, and we also found ways of solving problems concerning health and safety that the workers were dealing with in the plants.

The joint programs served an essential purpose with regard of progress within the automobile industry. The idea put forth by the UAW was genius, and the execution of that idea will forever be commended. I feel blessed to have been a part of it all. In fact, in my opinion, the joint programs were the single most important aspect of the progress concerning the relationship between the union and management, as well as supervisors and workers. I will admit that most of us in the union were quite wary of the idea at first, based solely on the history of the extreme turmoil between union and corporations. We figured that General Motors was pulling another fast one on us. I mean, you must understand that this was still a time that workers were not permitted to eat in the same cafeteria with management and supervisors. And this is just one of the examples of the obvious class lines drawn within auto plants. But as the joint programs began and workers started to receive help with problems, as well as better working conditions and job and wage security, it became apparent that the joint programs just might work.

I witnessed firsthand that they most certainly did. I had left a plant where workers and suits did not eat together, let alone congregate, and now I watched as union men and corporate men sat shoulder to shoulder and actually became friends. It was impossible not to see the progress.

My joint program, health and safety education and training, was completed in two years. I left my job with *the UAW International Union and returned to my plant in Marion, Indiana and began my work as a forklift driver. I was a respected man in the plant and I remained heavily active within the union, enjoying my work, my company, and all of the progress we had made and were still making.*

Chapter Seven

I returned from the UAW International Union back to my home plant in Marion, Indiana in 1990. I started work in my classification as a hi-lift driver on the third shift. The social and working climate had changed for the better in the two short years I was away from the plant. I credit that to the joint programs as well as the ongoing fight of the UAW to continue bettering the lives of workers as well as bettering the relationship between union and management. As I worked my job, I reminisced about my early days with General Motors. Thirty-four years had passed since I began working for GM and the changes I had seen were astounding. My early years as a union committeeman were filled with struggle and turmoil. Management did not respect the union back then, and, in turn, I think we had very little respect for them. There were definitely two distinct sides working against one another, but now, thirty years later, the line between those two sides had blurred tremendously. We worked together now, solving problems and compromising. That is not to say we agreed on everything because we most certainly did not, but even our disagreements were now being handled with respect and maturity.

The automobile industry had matured. The General Motors Corporation and its individual plants had matured. The UAW had become an undeniable force as important, if not more important, than the corporations themselves. We had fought for and earned our respect. As the nineties began and I did my job at the plant, I did not have any problems with my supervisors or management. In fact, they were going out of their way to assist me with any problems I was having with the job. I could not believe the difference between working at this time and working thirty-four years before. It was like night and day, and this is what I am talking about when I use the term "progress." We had progressed as an industry, we had progressed as a union, we had progressed as a corporation, and we had progressed as working class men and women.

As the decade of the 1990s began, the country was entering the end of the era of Reagan and Bush. It had been twelve long years of Republican rule and the economy, industry, the working class, and Americans in general were in need of change. The UAW was constantly at odds with the republican administration. Union members rallied together to protest the Persian Gulf War which we were in the midst of. They would rally together yet again come election time.

Campaigning hard against the re-election of George Bush, the UAW backed democratic candidate Bill Clinton. Although union members were unsure of how well Clinton and his administration would deal with industry and the union, it was clear that any change would provide improvement. Also, history had proven that the union thrived with a democratic president in office. President Bill Clinton was elected in a landslide vote in November 1992, and he began serving the country in 1993.

1993 was also the year that UAW President Owen Bieber retired and handed over the union reigns to the newly elected eight UAW President Stephen P. Yokich. Yokich had served five terms as Vice-President for the UAW in during which time he headed union departments at General Motors and Ford. He also headed Agricultural Implement and Organizing Departments. Yokich was a skilled tradeperson and displayed a lifelong commitment to the concerns and needs of other skilled trades workers by serving as director of the UAW Skilled Trades Department since 1980.

Like the UAW Presidents before him, Stephen Yokich would prove to be the perfect man for the time. He was strongly involved in the joint programs that were started in the eighties. He was extremely proud of these programs which he referred to as "people programs." Yokich had his hand in a number of innovative programs concerning issues such as education and training, joint health and safety, employee assistance, childcare assistance, elder care assistance, tuition assistance for workers and their children, and several more. Yokich's undying attention to these programs, as well as his strong commitment to the general evolution of the union and its workers, would be invaluable throughout the nineties. He understood that it was most definitely in the union's best interest (as well as American citizens in general) to build strong, long-term partnerships to both enhance and secure the future of workers, companies, and communities.

As we moved deeper into the nineties, it became apparent that we, as a union and as an industry, had progressed into different times. Corporations and the union were working together more than they were fighting one another. In fact, it seemed as though the battle between union and management had taken a back seat to the battle each was fighting with the government.

Yokich, like many UAW presidents before him, had taken office during yet another period of unprecedented challenges, politically and economically. Although, President Clinton was highly endorsed by the union, he and his administration were beginning to show a pattern of siding with multinational corporations over workers. It was becoming apparent that we were living in a capitalistic society that showed no signs of changing. The lines between democrat and republican were disappearing. The working class was beginning to realize that elections only provided them with the choice of the puppet on the left or the puppet on the right and that there was no escaping the rich get richer, poor get poorer aspect of living under capitalist rule.

UAW President Yokich recognized this as well as anyone. An experienced political activist, Yokich began to explore alternatives to major party presidential candidates and speak of the need for a third party U.S. President. At the same time, Yokich kept his eye on the prize, so to speak, concentrating on both the present and the future of the union and its workers. Despite any political or economical challenges, Yokich was well aware of the power of the union and utilized that power to continually benefit workers. Committed to a core vision of social unionism, he was extremely skilled at adapting to changing times and representing the union with force at the bargaining table. Yokich became well known for speaking out strongly on the social issues that affected not only workers, but all citizens, in this country and other countries as well. He advanced collective bargaining to another level, bargaining for more than just workers, but for workers' families and communities as well. As the nineties continued, Yokich's bargaining, and especially his active role within the political scope, would make him a beloved and extremely valuable UAW President.

As the nineties cruised along and I entered my sixties, I continued my work as a hi-lift driver and enjoyed the benefits of a worker with over thirty-five years of service. I continued to be extremely active within the union for it was at this time that I truly began to appreciate what we as a union had accomplished, how much I was benefiting from being part of the union, and how much I would benefit once I retired. We had made so much progress. Some of that progress came through the negotiation of the aged employee paid pension. This enables an old man to sit in peace in his rocker and smoke his pipe, possibly with a sore back, but most definitely with financial security to show for it. And this was not a gift from the private enterprise system. It was fought for and earned by the union as a fair payment for past labor. It was back in 1949 that rallying UAW members coined the slogan "Too old to work, too young to die." Benefits like this were the result of courage, sweat, bloodshed, perseverance, and hard bargaining by the men and women of the union.

I was very pleased to see Stephen Yokich elected UAW President. I knew him to be a committed activist and a brilliant speaker, and I knew that he was the man that the union needed for now and especially for the future. The past successes and achievements of our mighty union were only eclipsed by the great challenges of tomorrow. No one understood this better than Yokich, and he not only had the ability to recognize what was best for both the union and the community, he could take his ideas to the bargaining table and achieve success with his amazing negotiating skills. Yokich did a lot for us in the nineties. He negotiated contracts that not only had an immediate positive effect, but that will continue to have a positive effect for union members in the years and

decades to come. He could see the big picture and that
was what the union was all about.

By the 1990s, the union had grown to be as powerful within the economy and politics as the corporations it had sprouted from. The UAW had compiled a history of leaders that thought, fought, and achieved success. Their groundbreaking battles for equality had resulted in the improvement of a countless amount of lives. However, the union never rested on its rich history. In an everchanging industry, economy, political climate, and world, an everchanging and evergrowing union must exist. Current UAW President Stephen P. Yokich understood this and focused strongly on furthering the union to benefit the American working class as well as the rest of the world.

In the late nineties, Yokich negotiated landmark agreements for profit sharing, job security, employee involvement in product quality, health care, and retirement security. He was setting a new standard for collective bargaining. In 1998, Yokich won the approval of UAW delegates to create a new vice-president position to focus solely on organizing. New workers enter the automobile industry everyday. The result of the new vice-president position has been a revitalization of the union's efforts to recruit members in traditional UAW manufacturing industries.

Yokich was sometimes referred to as the UAW's first "hippie" president. He was a tireless activist as concerned, if not more concerned, with peace, equality, and simple fairness as he was with the economy and industry. In the 1980s, as director of the UAW Organizing Department, he led a campaigning to diversify the union. His campaigning resulted in the inclusion of Michigan state employees in the union. In 1999, Yokich set his sights on corporate CEOs and NAFTA, the North American Free Trade Agreement.

At the Automotive News World Conference held in Detroit in January of 1999, Yokich spoke to the audience about his extreme distaste for "executive compensation," directly addressing the "runaway salaries" that were being paid to top-level industry executives. He pointed out that at one hundred corporations in 1965, CEOs received forty-four times the salaries of a plant worker, and that today, they get paid three hundred twenty-six times as much as the common plant worker. Taking his point further, Yokich explained that the average CEO earns seven hundred twenty-eight times as much as a minimum-wage worker. This was at a time when low-paying jobs had become commonplace. Yokich went on to point out the fact that if the minimum wage had kept pace with CEO compensation, minimum-wage workers would be getting $41 an hour now. He stated, "I think it's time we make the CEOs competitive. In 1997, the Big Three (GM, Ford, and Chrysler) alone paid its top executives forty-nine million dollars." Keep in mind, that did not include stock options. "That was ten million dollars more than the previous year. Do you really think that's the competitive way?"

Yokich also took time to address his intense opinion concerning the North American Free Trade Agreement (NAFTA). "NAFTA has been an absolute exact disaster," he stated. "It hasn't been good for Canada, it hasn't been good for Mexico, and it hasn't been good for the United States. We now face a trade deficit of $281 billion. And Mexicans are not earning a living wage." Yokich attacked the system, stating, "we are taking advantage of a non-living wage country. We keep buying into this nonsense."

Even with his strong focus on foreign relations, President Yokich kept American workers as his number one priority. He addressed the plight of the working class at the conference, asking, "Wouldn't it be simpler if every American is entitled to a job, a home, and health care?" He pointed out that at this time in America, "people are making a basic choice between health care and eating." Yokich's observation was a poignant one. As we entered the new millennium, a majority of Americans had come to realize that we live in a country with an abundance of money - enough money, in fact, to feed, house, and clothe not only every American, but every human being in the world, ten times over at that. And yet we see this money, billions and billions of dollars, going to the defense fund and the top one percent of this country's citizens, namely corporate CEOs. We are in need of great change. How far we have come, and yet how far we still have to go. Yokich knew this, and as the leader of the powerful UAW, he knew that the change we needed to make would require both strong commitment and basic knowledge of our government and its intentions and actions. The union and American citizens, especially the working class, needed to become more politically active.

Later in 1999, Yokich led negotiations that would focus on this need for political activeness. In the UAW-Big Three negotiations, he fought for and won a paid day off for UAW members on Election Day. This was an ingenious way of increasing union participation in the American political process that resulted in greater voter turnout in the 2000 election and has received praise by both Democrats and Republicans.

Before the 2000 United States Presidential Election, Yokich began to speak out about our need for an alternate party President. He made it known that the UAW would be intensely exploring alternatives to major party presidential candidates. He knew well that the Republican party had never been more of a nemesis for the union and the working class. He observed through the nineties that the Democratic party, although not exactly a nemesis, was not taking a stand for American workers like it had in the past. President Yokich was furious over the current U.S.-China agreement on WTO accession and Clinton and Gore's positive stance on the agreement that could cause hundreds of thousands of Americans to lose their jobs. He pointed out that the government had once again sided with multinational corporations over the working class.

Yokich said in May of 2000, "America's working families need and deserve a president they can count on to stand with them on their tough issues, not just the easy ones. That's why we have no choice but to actively explore alternatives to the two major political parties. It's time to forget about party labels and instead focus on supporting candidates who will take a stand based on what is right, not what big money dictates. Supporting those who support us is our political agenda, not just a slogan." Yokich's views had consistently proved to be prophetic. These statements are filled with the same prophecy. For the union, the working class, and America itself to continue to progress, we all must recognize the need for change and have the courage to become active in making that change.

Shortly after retiring from his post as UAW President, Stephen P. Yokich suffered a stroke and passed away on August 16, 2002. Like the union leaders before him, his success, words, and life will forever be remembered and appreciated. His prophetic views concerning trade relations and, especially, the political process and state of our government should serve as great inspiration to us now as union members, as working class citizens, and as Americans.

In seventy years, from 1932 to 2002, the union had come from a barely acknowledged, completely disrespected organization to one of the strongest and most recognized organizations in the world. That is progress, and this progress is only overshadowed by the progress that is to come in the next seventy years. There is still so much to fight for and so much to accomplish and new obstacles appear everyday. The UAW has accomplished so much, but the fight for fairness and equality still goes on today. We now enter a time when it is vital that union members and all Americans take the initiative to become heavily involved in the political process of our country. We need to feed off the inspiration of our great leaders who stayed true to the UAW slogan, "Solidarity Forever," and come together to continue to right the wrongs of our nation because, for all of its progress, the United States still has a very long way to go.

Let the story of the UAW show that any man or woman, regardless of race or class, can make a difference in this world. May you go forth and make your difference.

As I worked my final years as a hi-lift driver, I looked back at everything I had accomplished and everything we had accomplished as a union. I felt proud and fulfilled by my time at General Motors. In 1995, at age sixty-three I retired with thirty-eight and a half years of service. I saw a tremendous amount of progress in those thirty-eight and a half years, all of it for the good of the working people of this country. The union is the cause of the American working men and women, the men and women whose livelihood depends on the skills of their hands and the strength of their backs. If it wasn't for the union, working people would be nothing more than slaves to large corporations. I, as a man with nothing more than a high school education, was able to make a great life for myself and my family in this country, and that is because of the union.

After I retired, I moved to Tennessee, near the beautiful Smoky Mountains. With my worklife at a stand still, I had time to look back at my years with the UAW and General Motors. I could see the overwhelming amount of progress that had been made over the past seventy years with the UAW and the automobile industry. It makes me proud to have been a part of it all.

I had been living in Tennessee for three months when I received a letter from the East Tennessee International Union Retired Workers Council drop-in center which was located in a Union Hall in Knoxville. The letter informed me that if I ever had any problems with the Supplemental Agreements regarding the Health Care Program and/or the Life and Disabilities Program, which were part of my General Motors benefits, that there were people at the Union Hall specifically designated to help with these problems. These people also helped retirees from Ford and Chrysler.

The East Tennessee International UAW Retired Workers Council was established and financed by the UAW International Union. Jobs in the Council were assigned to retirees. They are UAW Counselors and they assist other retirees with issues regarding pension and benefits. After reading the letter, I went to visit the Union Hall. I spoke with two Counselors about my thirty eight and a half years with General Motors and the Local 977 in Marion, Indiana. After we talked, the Counselors said they were in need of help and asked if I would be interested in taking a job with the Council, helping other retirees. I spoke to the Council President and he put me to work. I am so glad that I took this job. I work with great people and I meet retirees everyday that I am able to assist. This does my heart good. Some of these retirees are actually from my Local 977 back in Indiana. These are people that I represented years ago back in the plant as a Committeeman. It is wonderful to me that after so many years and moves from state to state that I am still representing some of the same people that I represented before we retired. To have this opportunity is a beautiful surprise to me. So now, retired and seventy years young, I still remain active in the union. This makes me proud.

The manifest destiny of the union is to balance the scales and to achieve economic justice and equality for the men and women who earn their living by the sweat of their brow. The men and women of the union marching under the battle flag of the UAW have made a mighty contribution to the working class, the industry and economy, the government, and society as a whole. The achievements of our past are only matched by the challenges of our future.

Tomorrow's working men and women will face a brighter future if we acknowledge the ideals of freedom and peace originally set forth by our forefathers. The UAW recognizes this and focuses strongly on efforts to forge new strength for democratic ideals and to encourage cultural education. The UAW emphasizes a strategy for peace, for construction rather than destruction, for disarmament rather than armament. All of the world should recognize the huge amount of progress made by the UAW and the automobile industry in just seventy years. Working together, they continue to accomplish everything they set out to. If the nations of this world could work together in this same way, we could see progress in the form of peace. This would be the greatest progress that could ever be made.

About the Authors

John Henry Jackson was born in Balkin, Kentucky in 1932. After graduating high school, he served four years in the United States Air Force, returning to southeast Kentucky in 1955. In October of 1956, he began working for the General Motors Corporation in a plant located in Hamilton, Ohio. A year later, he moved to Marion, Indiana where he would work the remainder of his thirty-eight and a half years with GM. Jackson served as a Union Committeeman for the UAW. He also worked as trainer and educator for the UAW International Union as part of the GM/UAW Health and Safety Program. He retired in 1995 and moved to east Tennessee with his wife, Zella. At age seventy, he still remains active with the UAW, working as a counselor for the East Tennessee International UAW Retired Workers Council, assisting other union retirees. This is Mr. Jackson's first book.

Jason Blair Trout is the grandson of John Jackson. Trout, a graduate of Ball St. University, is a musician/songwriter, political activist, and free lance writer. He currently records and tours with his band, the God Star Social.

www.ingramcontent.com/pod-product-compliance
Lightning Source LLC
Chambersburg PA
CBHW051438280526
45785CB00003B/1337